MW00335495

Unlocking the Writing Process

INSPIRING LESSONS AND STORIES TO GET YOU STARTED

By
Barbara Bush Forletta

Published by Tracy Rose Publishing at Kindle Direct Publishing

ISBN: 978-0-578-95438-7

Copyright © 2021 by Barbara Bush Forletta

All rights reserved. When using lessons, please credit Barbara Bush Forletta and *Unlocking the Writing Process* along with the copyright date.

Book Coach: Judith Cassis

Formatter: Jean Jegel

Cover Design: Alishonn Bonnett, Mooxworx.com

Disclaimer

The writing lessons provided in *Unlocking the Writing Process* are designed to give teachers and other users of the book information on how to advance students' abilities in the writing process. The process was developed through years of working with students of all ages and abilities.

Anecdotal stories have been used to illustrate what sometimes goes on in a classroom, and those stories are offered to help teachers new to the profession, or who have been there a while, understand they are not alone and that solutions are available. Names of students and identifying details in stories have been changed in order to protect privacy.

Permission is granted to copy and use the lessons provided in the book. Anecdotal stories may not be copied.

Any mistakes are mine and mine alone.

Barbara Bush Forletta

Dedication

This book is dedicated to my children, grandchildren and friends who always believed I had the words in me even though it took a while for them to come out.

Thanks to my children, Karen and Tom for helping me with wise suggestions, read-throughs and technical support. I love you very much!

To my friends who have also read through several versions of this book, I thank you for your support and suggestions.

I am also grateful to the teachers and administrators I worked with who thought my lessons and stories were inspiring and always said, "We can't wait to see your book!"

Special thanks to my aides through the years who helped me meet the needs of our students each and every day.

Some think those of us who teach are the wise ones. I think my students were also wise and I learned much from them. "Thank You!"

I owe deep gratitude to Judith Cassis for her wisdom, guidance and friendship throughout the process of getting my book in print. To the other members of The Golden Pen Writers Guild, thank you for listening to all my stories and encouraging me in this endeavor–I really couldn't have done it without you!

Barbara Bush Forletta

Table of Contents

Introduction

I was born in Pittsburg, Pennsylvania in 1943 during WWII. And yes, that makes me sort of old, but it also makes me want to share some of my stories about teaching with you, because I think it might help.

In my life I've lived in 26 different places. WWII and the Vietnam War were part of the reason, as my dad and then my husband were stationed in cities around the country. The places I've lived helped shape me and who I was going to be.

It's the same with you and your students. Where we live, the people we encounter and the experiences we have, give us a sense of who we are and what we want to do with our lives.

I ultimately decided, and was guided, to be a teacher and I took my job seriously. I wanted to help students have the best lives possible and did what I could to help them move beyond where they were when they came into my classroom, to something better when they left.

During my teaching years I figured out a way to help students who didn't like writing. I explain how I came to this process as I share some of those lessons in *Unlocking the Writing Process*.

Since I am a visual learner and many of my students were also visual learners, I learned to incorporate visual arts in most of my lessons, especially writing lessons.

Come with me into what was once my world of teaching and my desire to help students learn, flourish and be better writers.

Here is a humorous anecdote to get things going.

Jackson's Story

I had been teaching for nine years and experience had shown me the two weeks before Christmas were usually the most difficult, with students anxious to be on vacation and thinking about the holidays.

It was that time again and I was working very hard to keep my second-grade class *on task* as much as possible. One of my students, Jackson, informed me he had forgotten his lunch money and knowing I was a soft touch, asked if he could borrow a dollar. I told him to remind me just before lunch.

When the appropriate time came, I went to my purse and withdrew the dollar. Earlier that morning, Jackson had been telling me all about his mother's new job and how much she liked it. He said, "She earns money to buy things for the family."

As I held the dollar out for him to take, a look passed over his face. It was obvious he was processing something when he asked, "Mrs. Forletta, do you work?"

Forcing myself not to laugh, I replied, "Yes, I do. I teach."

Jackson pondered that information for a second and then said, "You get paid to teach? How much do they pay you?"

With a chuckle in my voice and a lighter spirit that would hopefully last me throughout the next two weeks, I answered, "Usually not enough Jackson, but today, just enough!"

How I Got Here

I think it's important to know that the experiences you bring with you to teaching can make you a teacher with a large bag of resources. As I've said earlier, the places I lived made an impact. So too were all the things that happened to me along the way. Here are a few of them. See if your experiences are similar.

The Bike Ride

It was a summer day a long time ago when two boys riding their bicycles asked a friend to ride along with them. They told her they were going to surprise someone. So, she got on her bike and rode with them. As they approached the raised porch of the little girl getting a surprise, they started chanting, "Deaf and Dumb, Deaf and Dumb!" and they crashed their bikes into the porch. The porch was on the front of a Quonset hut in Roger Young Village, Griffith Park, California. It was just after the end of WWII and the temporary home of many returning soldiers and their families.

I was that five-year-old girl on the ride along and I stopped my bicycle when they started their chanting. I somehow knew what those boys were doing was wrong, even though I wasn't sure what *Deaf and Dumb* meant. The two boys laughed as they rode their bikes away. A tall man came out on the porch to talk to me. He said he was the father of the girl the boys were chanting about. He thanked me for not crashing into the porch and told me his daughter was not dumb.

He said, "My daughter can't hear, so she is deaf, but she is very smart and is learning to talk with her hands, using signs for language." He told me a little more about his daughter and how she was learning to "speak" with her hands and understand what was being said to her by "reading" what the signs of people who spoke to her through sign language were saying to her.

I thought about that incident as I grew and was deciding what I wanted to do with my life. It took a while, but in my late 20's I started working on becoming a teacher. I think that incident and a few others along the way led me down the path to education.

When I was in high school my guidance counselor suggested I should probably become a secretary instead of going on to college. At the time I was having difficulty with math classes. His counseling set me back for a long time as I didn't feel smart enough to be a teacher.

And later, as I sat in my daughter's third grade classroom for an open house, I listened to her current teacher say, "I don't care if your children like me or not, I'm just here to teach them." While not all my students liked me throughout my years of teaching, I was certainly more effective if they did, and if I had earned their trust and respect.

Many of my students challenged me daily to teach them. They did this in ways they were not even aware of. They dared me to break through the barriers and walls they erected to protect themselves. They dared me to care about them when so many in their lives did not. They dared me to help them in spite of difficult behavior and to stay with them for the long haul. They dared me to believe it was possible to teach them.

In my teaching career, I started out as an elementary teacher. Eventually I taught junior high special education, elementary again, and finally at the high school level, I again taught special education at a continuation high school. I was able to teach all those levels because I went back to California State University, Northridge, while still teaching to earn my Special Education Credential. All the things I learned along the way helped me to better understand the students I was privileged to teach.

The Writing Process–How to Unlock It

By the time I was teaching at the high school level and working with students who had learning disabilities, I realized I needed to simplify the process so my students could access the skill of writing. I thought back on all the grades I'd taught from elementary to junior high school and took from those experiences the parts that some of my students thought too complicated and made it easier for them to understand.

What follows is my method of teaching writing. Use what works for you.

All students I worked with had the ability to be creative, but many had forgotten how.

Twila Tharp, the choreographer, said, "Living a creative life has the nourishing power that we normally associate with food, love, and faith."

She also believed, "…being creative is a full-time job with its own daily patterns and routine–a routine available to everyone."

I also believe those things and tried to incorporate creativity into my lessons by using art, which is very hands on and tactile as well as visual. From there I approached the writing.

Author Frank McCourt, best known for his book *Angela's Ashes*, said, "Kids have a great sense of wonder and awe and curiosity."

It is that sense of *wonder, awe and curiosity*, I tried to tap into, in order to direct my students toward learning and writing.

I always started with a daily journal entry/writing prompt. It related to our current area of study, world events or personal reflection. A lesson format on journaling follows shortly.

I was the only one to read student journals. Anything they said was accepted and private unless in their journals they threatened someone, themselves, or if they were being threatened or harmed by someone else. In this case, they knew I would notify administrators and get help for them. That was the rule.

Each journal entry focused on writing fluency. Grammar, punctuation and spelling would be addressed in other written work. I never corrected the journal, just made comments about their entry as I wrote back to them. This could be time consuming, but the students looked forward to reading what I had written, which encouraged them to keep writing. Remember, I was going for fluency. The following chart is important to share with your students as they begin the process:

Important Things to Know

(A version of this worksheet is in the Appendix)

Parts of an Essay in Three Paragraphs

1. Explain to your readers what you are going to tell them. What is the essay about? This is the **Introduction.**
2. Give information about the subject. This is the **Body** of the essay.

3. Tell the reader what you told them. You are restating or summarizing. You can add something personal here if it relates to the essay. This is the **Conclusion**.

As students become familiar with this simple approach to writing, add more to the process until you end up with this version:

Parts of an Essay–Detailed Version

1. **Introduction**: Explain to the reader what you are going to tell them in an opening paragraph. At the end of the introduction, introduce your *Thesis*. This is the main focus. It is an idea or feeling about the topic/subject. You will support the *Thesis* with details and facts in the body of the essay.
2. **Body**: Give detailed information. Have at least three paragraphs, but more is better. This is an extension of the *Thesis*.
3. **Conclusion**: Tell the reader what you told them. You are restating or summarizing. This is a good place for personal observation or reflection about the topic/subject if it applies to your essay.

The Secret

Here is the *secret* for making it work: Start with lots of writing, including journals every day, which I've already mentioned. Have a writing folder for the students so they can put all their writing and any handouts relating to their writing, in the folder. It gives them ownership.

When you are ready for students to write about a topic, introduce the **Parts of an Essay** from above and the worksheet in the **Appendix**. This is where the drafts come in. Students want to complete their work in one draft and they are shocked when told they are going to have to write more. Get ready for many sighs and complaints. Ask students if they are familiar with the book *Charlotte's Web* by E. B. White. It's about a pig named Wilbur and an unusual friendship with a spider named Charlotte. Students might know it from their childhood. E. B. White wrote and rewrote the book many, many times. Share this information with your students to encourage them that rewrites are important. It gives them their best writing.

This next part is more work for you, the teacher, but it is important and ultimately creates better writers.

Students make an appointment with you. Have a sign-up sheet available and call each student to your desk to meet privately with you. At that time, have the student read their draft aloud. If they see or think they see a mistake, have them underline or circle it. Go back over the essay and help them find any errors they missed. Now, it is time for the student to rewrite the essay. Again, they meet with you and read their work out loud. Ask them if there are ways to make the essay better. As their teacher, make suggestions and send them off for another rewrite until the product is ready for final draft. This might sound tedious, but remember it works!

Students should type their final product on a computer and print it out.

Remember, writing is the demonstration of what a student understands.

Here is the rest of the **secret** for getting more writing from your students: Post all work, including rough drafts, stapled to the back of the final draft, on your bulletin boards.

Post or display all art work related to the written subject on or near the bulletin board. Students love to see their work around the room.

Lessons in this book are intermingled with stories from my experiences teaching. I start with the simpler lessons and move to more difficult lessons as students advance in their ability to write.

Pictures of art work associated with the subject matter are included after most lessons, providing an integrated experience of how the visual arts lead to better written work. You can come up with additional ideas from your own bag of tricks to enrich the lessons so your students will want to write!

If they can see it and they can say it, then with practice and work, they can write it!

Note: Lessons 1-5 are designed to be used in order to lay the foundation for establishing a good writing process. Lessons 6 and beyond can be used in any order to further develop the students' writing skills.

General Rubric

For Grade of A:

Student participates in all activities assigned. Reading, Writing, Discussion, Projects. Student demonstrates complete understanding of all concepts and facts of each activity. Student asks for help when needed and engages teacher and aides in discussion of assignments.

For Grade of B:

Student participates in all activities assigned. Reading, Writing, Discussion, Projects. Student demonstrates an above average understanding of concepts and facts of each activity.
Student asks for help and clarification of assignments as needed.

For Grade of C:

Student participates in all activities assigned. Reading, Writing, Discussion, Projects. Student demonstrates a basic understanding of the concepts and facts of each activity. Student occasionally asks for help or may turn down help when offered.

A variety of other resources for each assignment should be available as an alternative for completion of work based on the student's ability.

Any grade below a C is not acceptable and the work must be re-done.

*Check with your district or school to see if there is a Rubric that all students need to attain. This is important if your special needs student is mainstreamed to a regular classroom for part of the day. Use the appropriate Rubric.

Core Curriculum Standards

The lessons in *Unlocking the Writing Process* were developed using California State Standards. They are referred to as Common Core State Standards. Common Core State Standards can be found online at http://corestandards.org/ELA-Literacy

Overview

Key Features of Reading are text complexity and the growth of comprehension:
> Increased text complexity
> Connections among ideas and between texts
> Sensitivity to inconsistencies, ambiguities and poor reasoning

Key Features of Writing are text types, responding to reading and research:
> Developing writing types: argumentative, informative/explanatory narratives
> Students draw upon and write about evidence from literary/informational texts
> Planning, revising, editing and publishing

Key Features of Written and Oral English Language Conventions:
> Understanding words and phrases, their relationships and nuances
> Acquiring new vocabulary–general academic and domain specific words/phrases

Key Features of Listening and Speaking:
> Learning to work together, express and listen to ideas
> Integrating information for oral, visual, quantitative, and media sources
> Evaluating what was heard and adapting speech to context and task

All lessons utilize some or all of the above Core Curriculum Standards depending on length and depth of the lesson.

Teachable Moments

Writing opportunities can happen at any time. Once in a while there are those *Teachable Moments*. Maybe something happens in the world and you do an impromptu lesson on the geographical area where it occurred. Or, Joe breaks a leg while playing basketball during PE and the students want to know what will happen because an ambulance came and took him away. This really did happen in my class so we researched anatomy, broken bones and healing times.

Here's another example of a moment that happened in my classroom. It hadn't rained for quite a while in Southern California. The weather report for that day predicted the possibility of thunder showers–you know how that goes–it usually doesn't happen and often didn't even though the forecasters said it would. Well, on that day, it happened!

Students were working quietly on assignments when there was a loud boom. Everyone sat up looking around thinking, *earthquake*, or *plane crash*? The school was located near an airport. The pounding sound on the roof and lightning out the window gave it away.

"I guess it must be rain." A student named Johnny called out.

Not only was it rain, lightning and thunder, but also golf ball size hail. Students flocked to the windows to watch and listen. Here was the teachable moment!

Have a quick discussion about weather. Students can orally share about the last time they saw heavy rain.

Do a quick journal entry and have them write a short story about something rain related, like playing in the rain, or their dog getting lost because of the thunder and being scared and running away.

It's important to grab on to those moments. Let it be okay to skip a few minutes of math or language while you go with what interests the students in the moment.

You'll find it's also a bonding experience with your class which can be more precious than the missed lesson because of taking the time to share your stories and interact with them, as they interact with you. Take advantage of the here and now!

When this happened in my classroom so many years ago, as the students rushed to the window to watch nature in all its glory, the sight of them imprinted itself on my memory. When I researched the cover for this book, I decided I wanted one to represent that experience because it demonstrated my philosophy of seizing the moment to teach a lesson and write about it.

Lesson 1: Daily Journal

Background

Students who are learning disabled have often given up on regular classroom activities that involve writing because it can be difficult for them. Even regular education students might disagree with writing a daily journal, but it lays the groundwork for strengthening all writing.

Objective

Students will become comfortable with daily writing in their personal classroom journal and occasional oral sharing of journal topics when appropriate.

Core Standards

Production and Distribution of Writing.
Presentation of Knowledge and Ideas.
Expressing and Listening to Thoughts and Ideas.

Materials Needed

Pen or pencil, classroom journal.

Instruction

This is a daily writing activity. It should be used each day and the journal topic should be posted on the board before students enter. That way they know to get their journal, sit down and start writing.

1. Journal: Have students write on a specific prompt. For example: List things you see in the classroom. Set a time limit appropriate for your students–I usually allowed about five minutes.

   Examples of simple topics:

   Things I want for Christmas/Chanukah/Kwanza…
   Things able to fit in a shoebox…

Nine words describing me are…

Things in a car…

Things that make me angry/happy…

Five favorite colors…

Foods I like to eat are…

Or, a more serious topic like…"Things happening in [a particular place in the United States or the world…] make me feel…because…"

There are many books and online sites available on journal topics. I would sometimes have a student chose the topic if there was something on their minds.

2. Using journals, and assigning a thought-provoking topic, have students write for a full five minutes. Encourage students to write for the whole time–this develops *muscle memory*. When students don't know what to write, tell them to write, "I don't know what to write." They eventually get tired of writing that statement and find something else to write about, hopefully the topic assigned. Their pencil should not leave the paper. To make things fun, teacher should participate in the five-minute journaling assignment.

Art Collage

Michelle was about 16 when she first came into my class. She would never write in spite of my best enticements to do so. However, she loved to talk about her wedding. Understand, she was only 16, did not have a boyfriend let alone a fiancé, but was preoccupied with her future wedding. It was all she could think or talk about.

I had many old magazines in my classroom. One day I said, "Why don't you do a collage about what you'll wear on your wedding day?"

Michelle loved browsing through the magazines I had in my classroom, so decided that was a great idea! I actually went out and bought some bridal magazines for her too. Soon enough Michelle presented me with a beautiful collage of how she would appear on her special day.

In fact, she was so taken by the experience she wanted to make another one about her imaginary groom-to-be, the reception and the carriage with the white horse that would carry the newly married couple to their party.

This was what I had been hoping for! Here was my *ah ha* moment as her teacher.

I said, "Before you can do another collage, I want you to describe to me what you see in the pictures, the collage."

Her oral language was good and she was able to describe it very well.

I told her, "Now, write it all down. Write down everything you just told me."

Still resistant to writing, it took a day or two for her to get to it. Her desire to do another collage was stronger, so I had her!

When she finished, I helped her refine the piece using the **Important Things to Know**. Then away she went on her next collage and her next written description.

It was the start she needed to break her barrier against writing.

Here's the most interesting part; A few years after she graduated from high school, my instructional aides and I were invited to Michelle's wedding.

It was just as envisioned in those collages and the written descriptions–right down to the carriage and white horse!

Take time to find out what interests each and every student in your classroom. In Michelle's case, it was her future wedding and all that went with it. Use their interests to pull your students into the learning and writing process.

Another student I worked with only liked to read *graphic novels*. When it was time to do book reports, Richard didn't want to read the books assigned so I had him bring in one of his *graphic novels* to use for the book report. This got him writing and eventually reading some of the books I assigned, as well as doing those book reports.

So, tap into the interests of your students and see how having them do things that interest them personally can help you transition them into your curriculum.

Teacher Notes

Lesson 2: Topic Sentences

Background

Many students are visual. Remember the student in the previous story talk about her wedding? She didn't want to write? Well, after making a collage and seeing her dreams visually, she was able to write about it.

Objective:

Students will write a description of a picture, select a topic sentence and revise written drafts to improve the sequence of writing.

Core Standards

Production and Distribution of Writing.
Comprehension and Collaboration.

Materials Needed

Pencils, old magazines, paper.
Classroom writing folder to keep unfinished work in for later access.

Instruction

This lesson takes approximately one week.

1. Instruct students to find a picture of interest to them from one of the magazines. Tell them to consider the following questions:

   Where do you think the picture is located?
   Why do you think the artist/photographer selected this picture?
   What is the picture about?
   Who is in the picture?
   Describe the different shapes, colors, and textures in the picture.

2. Now that the students have considered the above questions, instruct them to write a description of what they see. Have them write without thinking about perfection. Getting the words down on paper is the main goal. *This is a rough draft.* This also ties in with the fluency worked on in the journal writing.

3. Instruct students to look at what they've written. Have students pick a sentence summing

up what the whole picture is about and underline the sentence. This should be their topic sentence. *A topic sentence tells what the paragraph is all about in a very short way without all the details.*

4. Meet with the student and go over what they have written so far. If need be, review the section in **Important Things to Know**–specifically the **Secret** part talking about the process of meeting with the student.

5. Ask the student to rewrite their description of the picture, which is now in the form of a paragraph, based on your meeting with them. Students write the paragraph again, correcting the mistakes they found on their own and with your help.

6. Meet with the student again to review their final written work. Students should complete written work on computer and print it out. They should make an extra copy to put in their writing folder for future reference on topic sentences.

7. Have students glue or staple their picture to an 8x10 piece of tag board along with their written work.

8. To incorporate oral language into the lesson, have students pair up and share their selected pictures and written paragraphs. This also helps students become comfortable talking and sharing with others. The practice will support students gaining skills towards oral presentation in front of the whole class.

9. Place the completed work on the bulletin board.

Lesson 3: Reading Comprehension and Vocabulary Development

Background

Although the book, *Tuck Everlasting* by Natalie Babbitt, is mainly for grades 4-8, the concept of eternal life, friendship, honor and trustworthiness applies to older students as well. Many students who have difficulty writing also have difficulty reading because of dyslexia or other processing problems. This book with a lower reading level, but high in interest, can help improve reading and vocabulary.

Objective

Students will strengthen comprehension skills and vocabulary acquisition.

Core Standards

Phonics and Word Recognition.
Level and Range of Reading.
Level of Text Complexity.
Integration of Knowledge and Ideas.

Materials

The book, *Tuck Everlasting*, one copy for each student if possible.
Poster board, construction paper, art supplies, pens, pencils, journals, writing folders.
Real, hand-held dictionaries–these can be shared, one per two students. I know students can use programs online to check for word definitions, but looking up words in a dictionary is a good skill to have, in my opinion!
Online resources relating to this book.

Instruction

The following lessons took approximately four weeks.

The focus of each lesson was determined chapter by chapter and the discussions were generated by the text. Vocabulary words were selected from each chapter. Some words are presented for you on the next page, but feel free to use words chosen by you.

1. Talk to the students about the meaning of the words *lifetime*, *forever*, and *everlasting*. When you feel you have had adequate discussion and students have defined the words

appropriately, ask them to write about "living forever" as a journal entry.

2. Journal: Do you think you would like to live forever? What does the statement "living forever" mean to you?

3. After reading the prologue, chapters 1-3, discuss *foreshadowing*. Using their journals and dictionaries, have students find the definition for *foreshadowing* and write it down.

4. Have students work in pairs looking for *foreshadowing* in those chapters. Students gather as a group again and share what they felt were examples of *foreshadowing*.

5. Continue reading each chapter together. Sometimes the teacher reads and students follow and sometimes ask for student volunteers to read. After each chapter, pick vocabulary words you feel your students need to learn. Also discuss events of each chapter.

   The following vocabulary words are ones I chose. Feel free to use these or any others of your choosing.

abruptly	everlasting	oppressive
axis	exasperated	peculiar
barbarian	faltered	perversely
beaming	forlorn	petulance
bovine	galling	plaintively
brooch	gingerly	poised
cautiously	gnat	prologue
clung	grimace	remnant
comprehend	gurgled	rueful
consoling	housed	scornful
consolingly	illiterate	seized
constable	immense	seldom
creased	infinite	self-deprecation
devote	intrusion	surge
disheartened	jaunty	tarnish
earnestly	loft	threadbare
envious	melancholy	weep
epilogue	midst	wisp

6. Students answer the following questions in their journals or use the questions as a mini quiz to see if the students are understanding the story and its concepts.

Compare and contrast Winnie before the kidnapping and after. How is she the same or different?

Are there any characters that are most like you? Which ones and why?

Make a list of the pros and cons, positive and negative, reasons for living forever.

Pretend you have found an answer to Tuck's problem of living forever. Write about your solution and tell why you think it will work.

When Winnie finds Jesse at the magic spring, Mae gasps, "The worst is happening at last" Do you agree or disagree with her? Why or why not?

7. Art Project: Students should consider the following; the Tuck family is wanted for kidnapping. Design a **Poster** with all the important/pertinent information.

8. Divide the class into groups, depending on the size of your class. Each group works together to answer questions. Develop the questions while going through the book based on the interests of your students. When done, groups reassemble and share answers. Have the groups select a secretary to take notes and a spokesperson to share the answers. Secretary can do both.

9. Finish reading the book, asking students to read aloud and taking turns with the teacher. If students aren't familiar with certain words, tell them to write the words in their journal to be discussed after the reading is completed.

10. Art Project: Students will pick a scene from the book to recreate as a **Setting Poster**. Students can use pictures from magazines, their own drawing and anything else creative to complete their art work. Art work is shown on next page.

11. When the poster is complete, have students write a description of the poster. Description should include what they chose and how the poster represents that choice. They should use the method of writing an essay in **Important Things to Know**. Then have students make an appointment with you to go over their rough drafts. Have them circle or underline words they think are misspelled as they read their work aloud to you. Go over it again and make suggestions for improving the work. Meet again until draft is ready to be written out on the computer and printed. Display all written work with rough drafts stapled to back. Include **Poster** and **Setting Poster** next to written work.

12. Tuck Everlasting Quiz: Have students answer the following questions on a separate sheet of paper.

1. Use each of the following words in a complete sentence:
    ponderous, profoundly, wistful—other forms of the word are acceptable.
2. List the main characters in the book.
3. What is the setting of the story?
4. List the parts of this word: Unwittingly. Use these terms; base word, suffix, prefix.
5. Describe the conflicts in chapters 20, 21, and 22. Identify each type of conflict.
6. How does the conflict of the story create an interesting tale?
7. Now that you know the story and how it ended, what would you have done if you had been Winnie? Why?

Example of artwork.

Remember, the reason for the art work is so the students can "see" the story visually and write about it. Writing is the main goal here. Some of the art work is exceptional and some just so, depending on the skill of the students. But all art work is spectacular because of the creative nature of doing it!

Doing What You Need to Do

In order to advance to another pay level in the field of highly paid educators–*just kidding about the highly paid part*–we have to take additional courses throughout the years. One of the best courses I ever took was a week-long art class. I was teaching in Nevada at the time and it was during summer break.

The class was held at the local two-year college in one of the art rooms. When we arrived, the room was empty except for tables and chairs. As I remember, there were about 15 of us in the room including the teacher. We didn't know what to expect and I was nervous because art is not one of my strengths. Music, yes, art, no. When I was in junior high school, I was exempted from art class so I could be in glee club. I was glad at the time, but years later realized I should have taken the art class.

Instead of just talking about art, the teacher taught us how to do art. In other words, she introduced the lesson, gave us the supplies we needed and told us to create. Create we did, even me. We did collages, drawings in black and white, a shoe box diorama, torn paper art and many, many other projects. By the end of the week, the once empty room was alive with all our projects adorning the walls and desk tops. Our room looked like a beautiful, colorful art museum. That week of art, as well as advancing my pay, was by far the most fun experience I ever had in an extracurricular class.

That week I learned to appreciate the process of doing art. Seeing, hearing and doing are three modalities that help us understand the world around us.

 From that point on, I incorporated art into all my lessons because I felt more confident in my ability and wanted students to feel confident too. Visual arts in science, in language arts, in social science, and even in mathematics is important. Because if you can draw it, diagram it and visually put it down on paper, it's easier to understand.

The next year one of my students in 2nd grade didn't like me at all. Sara probably didn't like herself very much either. She let me know of her dislike almost daily by sticking her tongue out whenever I glanced her way. She wasn't fond of following directions and quite disruptive to the other students. However, the one thing that interested her was art and because I had taken that art class, I was able to help her through art projects. If I could incorporate art in a lesson, she was much more agreeable to learning.

My classrooms now used every bulletin board and the top of every clear surface to display the student's art and their written work, especially at the high school level with my learning-disabled students. Many of them had never had their work displayed and they enjoyed seeing it on bulletin boards where all who entered could see and appreciate it. They even liked looking at the other student's work too.

Try using art projects along with, and relating to, other subjects in your classroom and see how it enriches everything you do with your students. Some students are left brained, which is more verbal, analytical, and orderly. It deals with reading, writing and computations. The right brain is more visual and intuitive. It deals with imagination, arts, non-verbal cues, as well as intuition and rhythm. Combining the two brains during your lessons will give students who excel in one or the other the ability to experience learning in a different way. You will be more creative as you plan your lessons and your classroom will reflect that creativity.

Lesson 4: Using Resources: Artists, Their Work and Biographies

Background

This lesson deals with great artists. There are many books on artists and many resources to choose from. I chose a series that was simple and featured a variety of artists. Find the series that works for you. Remember, many students are reluctant to do any kind of research because of difficulty with reading.

Objective

Students will become familiar with the use of a variety of resources relating to art and artists. They will then use the information they found to write about their artist.

Core Standards

Integration of Knowledge and Ideas.
Key Ideas and Details.
Production and Distribution of Writing.
Research to Build and Present Knowledge.

Materials Needed

Pen, pencil, paper, colored pencils and markers.
Teacher's choice: simplified books about artists–check online resources.
Plain paper for art project and tracing paper if needed.
Book report form of teacher's choice. (See **Appendix** for form if needed.)

Instruction

This lesson can take up to three weeks to complete, or as long as your students need.

1. Journal: Have students answer the following questions in their journals:
    Do you think art is important? Why or why not?
    If you have a favorite artist, who is it?
    Can you draw? Do you know someone who can?
    Tell about your art or the art of another person you know.

2. At some point if students bring up graffiti as art, have a discussion about that topic, acknowledging the artistic nature of that art form and artists who do graffiti. Bring the

discussion back to the artists in the books you are using and the time periods represented.

3. Have students pick a book about one artist. Ask them to skim through the book. This helps foster interest. Students should start reading on their own. The books I chose had some illustrations done as cartoons. This helped grab student's attention. If students need help with reading, work with them individually.

4. Ask students to take notes regarding their selected artist as they read through the book using these starting points:

   Artist's family
   Date of birth
   Place of birth
   Style of art
   Success as an artist

5. Instruct students to pick one of the works of art in the book to reproduce in the artist's style. Student may draw freehand to copy the art or use tracing paper to trace the art.

6. Using colored pencils, students color their work of art. On the computer, or paper, students write and describe the work of art, the artist's style, when the work was completed by the artist and any further information of interest. *This is a rough draft.*

7. Have students go online and research the artist they picked. Again, students take additional notes from online information.

8. Using a book report form, have students use the information they've gathered to start working on an outline for their report. See **Appendix** for book report form.

9. Students meet with teacher to talk and read through their outline and notes. Based on meeting with the teacher, students write the first draft of their report and again meet with the teacher. Now, students correct mistakes and rewrite their report. Another way to get the information on paper is to have students write a biography of the artist instead of a book report. Your choice.

10. Once reports are corrected, completed and typed, students meet with a partner and share

their art and reports. It is important all rough drafts are kept together with the final report so students can see the progress they've made in their writing. Staple rough drafts to back of final draft. Post all written reports and art on bulletin board.

Here are some of the artists my students did reports on:

Mary Cassatt
Leonardo DaVinci
Frida Kahlo
Salvador Dali
Francisco Goya
Michelangelo
Claude Monet
Georgia O'Keeffe
Pablo Picasso
Rembrandt
Diego Rivera
Vincent Van Gogh

Here is some of the work done by students.

The Power of Unusual Methodology

My high school class had just started working on a unit called *Artists; Their Work and Biographies*. I had a new student who arrived a few days earlier with quite the attitude. Josh disliked being sent to a continuation high school and demonstrated his dismay each and every day.

It usually took about two weeks for students to settle in. I was there to help them and get them back to the regular high school if they so desired. It hadn't yet been two weeks for Josh.

On this particular day, our classroom had additional students as a favor to the teacher across the hall who had an ASB–Associated Student Body—meeting and needed to find a place for his 6th period students. The visiting teacher placed them at three different tables, making sure students who had problems with each other were at separate tables. My aides were sitting at tables one and two. I was at a third table with students, including the new boy. Josh was working on a Contemporary Issues contract where he looked through newspapers, finding specific assigned articles and writing about them.

Having come across pictures showing models in an underwear advertisement, Josh elbowed the student next to him, and made some inappropriate remarks.

I quietly said, "Move on."

Turning the page, he found another picture that he inappropriately described to his neighbor.

Again, I said, "Move on."

His response was, "I hate this ******* school!"

He glared at me, threw the paper down and stood.

I responded with, "If you don't ******* move on, I'm going to walk you down the ******* hall to the principal's office where she will ******* suspend you."

He hesitated a moment, sat down and agreed to move on.

Because Josh was somewhat of an artist himself, the unit on artists eventually drew him into being at our school and becoming part of our student body. Josh stayed to graduate from our school.

Sometimes unusual techniques worked, as did the one described above. In today's classrooms where students have phones that take videos, I wouldn't have done or said what I did. You'll need to find your own way of dealing with difficult situations. Each situation is different and requires your ability to think on your feet to get the best results for the success of your student.

Oh, and by the way, I let the teacher from across the hall know he might be getting calls from parents regarding my language. The next day after school I asked if that had happened.

He said, "No, but my students wanted to come to your classroom again today!"

Lesson 5: Character Development

Background

Gaining the ability to understand oneself is important for students. Using real and fictional characters for comparison often encourages and helps self-understanding. J. M. Barrie wrote *Peter Pan* for the Llewellyn Davies boys. He unofficially adopted them and became their mentor after their parents died. More information about this is available online to help with preparation of the lessons.

Objective

Students will understand the concept of character development and *comparison/contrast* as they read the book *Peter Pan* by J. M. Barrie.

Core Standards

Integration of Knowledge and Ideas.
Research to Build and Present Knowledge.
Craft and Structure.
Text Types and Purposes.
Choosing Language that Expresses Ideas Precisely and Concisely.

Materials

Copy of the above-named book for each student.
Journal, pen, pencils, colored pens and pencils, blank sale tags with strings, non-toxic paint.
Small boxes in a variety of shapes available at craft stores–4 to 6 inches across.
Craft items for *Time Capsule Art Project*: paint, pipe cleaners, beads, feathers, sparkles, construction paper and any other items you think necessary for lesson.
Access to online research.
Movies dealing with above book to view for *comparison/contrast* and use of *poetic license* as the story line changed with some of the movies.

Instruction

The following lessons took approximately seven weeks to complete.

1. Query students on their familiarity of the story *Peter Pan* and any movies they might have seen relating to the book.

2. Journal: What do you know about the story of *Peter Pan*? The main character, Peter,

taught the children to fly. What would it be like to fly?

3. Read the book with the students, starting out reading aloud to them while they follow along. This helps with word recognition. As reading progresses, ask students to start identifying with a character most like themselves. Continue reading each day, asking students to volunteer to read, as well as teacher reading to students. This continues over the course of the weeks needed to complete the lessons and visual arts projects.

4. Depending on the movies you've selected that relate to the book, make sure you have permission from the parents/guardians to view parts of the movies dealing with the character development of the main characters. There is a form in the **Appendix** to use for permission.

5. Journal: Which character did you most identify with in the book and in the movies? List the similarities and the differences between you and the character you picked. There is a worksheet called **What Do We Have in Common?** at the end of the lessons. Students will transfer the information they have in their journals onto this worksheet at a later date. See step 13.

6. The term *poetic license* refers to the ability of a writer to alter a story line. Discussion: Ask students the following, Was *poetic license* used in the movies? How was it done? Give examples.

7. In the book, Peter said, "Think about a 'happy thought' that could make you fly." Journal: If you were able to have a 'happy thought' that could enable you to fly, what would that thought be and where would you go?

8. Using the results from the above journal, have students use a variety of websites for research. Students then print out a map of their flight and destination, as well as a fact sheet about the place they want to fly to. Examples: www.mapquest.com/atlas or www.cia.gov/cia/publications/factbook.

9. Now that students have their information, it's time to write about it. Using the **Parts of an Essay** worksheet from previous lessons, have students write a short essay about where they want to go and why. Have students make appointment with you to go over rough draft as before. Continue this method until final draft is ready to be typed out on the computer.

10. Students will now use their writing, printed map, fact sheet and short completed essay to create a poster about where in the world they would fly. Feel free to use the shadow figures from the visual arts project at the end of the lessons.

11. *Time Capsule Art Project*: Students pick a craft box of choice for project. They will use the character they most identified with to develop the items for the capsule–have students refer to journals. Have them decide on five items that best represent their character. The items could be pictures from magazines or something they draw. For example, a feather to represent the feather on Peter's hat or anything they like. Small sale tags can be used to identify the items. Have students get creative as they paint and decorate their craft box using paint, colored pencils, beads and anything available in your classroom to complete their project.

12. For the writing assignment, have students get their capsule and take out the five items. Exploring items, the shape of the box, the color and texture of the things they selected, and the reasons why, have students write about their capsule. Using the same writing technique and meetings with teacher, have students type up the completed essay.

13. Now have students complete the **What Do We Have in Common?** worksheet. At the bottom of worksheet, have students write what their differences are too.

14. Place all essays, art projects and *Time Capsules* on bulletin boards or table tops for viewing. Hopefully, by now your room looks like a mini art museum!

Example of art project follows.

What Do We Have in Common?

Me   My Character

What Things About Us Are Different?

Me   My Character

Teacher Notes

Lesson 6: Internment Camps

Background

Some students may experience racism and prejudice in one form or another. In today's day and age, it's important to help students understand their feelings of fear or uncertainty when it comes to perceived differences in others. The experience by the author of *Farewell to Manzanar,* Jeanne Wakatsuki Houston, can help students understand that what happened in the past shouldn't happen in the future and shouldn't happen now. Manzanar is in the Mojave Desert not far from where I taught these lessons. Some students remember driving by the site on Highway 395. The proximity made the reality of the story more impactful to them.

Objective

By reading the book *Farewell to Manzanar* by Jeanne Wakatsuki Houston & James D. Houston, students will develop an understanding of the complexities of war. They will research the reasons nations and people select and attack various groups based on fear. They will also explore reasons for racism and anger toward Asian Americans because of the Covid-19 Pandemic.

Standards

Research to Build and Present Knowledge.
Production and Distribution of Writing.
Integration of Knowledge and Ideas.
Range of Reading.
Historical and Social Sciences Analysis Skills used include:
    Chronological and Spatial Thinking
    Research, Evidence, and Point of View
    Historical Interpretation

Materials

If possible, each student should have a copy of the book.
With permission of the school and the parents, the movie of same title, Universal Television/Educational, 1976.
Journals, pens, pencils, colored pens, tag board.
Access to computers and online resources.
Information on Japanese Sand Gardens and Haiku Poetry available online.
Empty shoe boxes, sand, plastic forks used as rakes, rocks, various materials to create a Sand Garden.

Instruction

The following lessons took approximately four weeks.

1. Using their journals, have students write down information they know about WWII. Students then share aloud different facts as teacher writes comments on the board–it's interesting to see if any students come up with internment camps for Japanese Americans. This opens the discussion about Manzanar. Direct the discussion toward this time in our history. If students don't mention internment camps, add this to the generated list about WWII since this is the focus of the lesson.

2. Ask students if they talk about racism and prejudice with family and friends. Ask if they see it in the news, on television, or any other social media sites. Discuss with students the meaning of stereotype. The dictionary says stereotype is "an oversimplified opinion or belief about a person, group or event–lacking individuality."

   Make a handout with a list of different groups–see suggestions below.

   Have students write two things they believe about each group that could be considered stereotyping. Add to the list any groups you feel important for discussion.

   Various Ethnicities
   LGBTQ+
   High School Social Groups
   Religions
   Men/Women
   Senior Citizens
   Politicians
   Teenagers

   As teacher, chart those things students believe about the above on the board as students call out their responses. Not all stereotypes are negative. It's interesting to see what your students might say.

3. In their journals, have students define the terms *Setting, Irony,* and *Conflict.* These terms will help students understand the place and time written about in the book. The terms also help students develop a greater understanding of the main character of the book as

she tells her story.

This might also be a good time to talk and write about the Covid-19 Pandemic regarding Asian Americans because of the misinformation regarding the cause of the pandemic. **Compare** and **Contrast** are further terms to have students define as they dig into these topics.

4. Begin reading the book a chapter at a time, having students volunteer to read aloud. If each student does not have a book, have them share. As the teacher, read occasionally to the students. Students should jot down important or interesting information from the book in their journals, citing page numbers for future reference.

   Discuss each chapter when completed, and as teacher, write down important thoughts for later discussion.

5. When book is finished, show the movie mentioned in **Materials**. Students should take notes in their journals during viewing. Notes will be used along with other information for a final essay.

6. Have students do online searches for articles about other camps like Manzanar and write about their findings. Also, have them search for old articles/stories from WWII and discuss their feelings about what happened.

7. There are many resources available regarding this time period in history. Look for any resource you think will add to this study so your students can fully understand how and why Japanese Americans were put in internment camps. Create journal topics based on the materials you use.

8. Sand Gardens offered the people of Manzanar a way to create a place of peace and familiarity in a setting far from that reality. As an art project, collect shoe boxes–many shoe stores will give you empty boxes. Have students bring in rocks and various other materials to design their own garden. Do research online about creating a small Sand Garden and then let the students be creative with their own gardens.

9. Haiku is a poetic form and type of poetry from the Japanese culture. Find examples of Haiku poetry online to share with your class. Study the different types of Haiku and pick one type to have your students compose.

Here's one I wrote using 4-5-4 syllables:

Sweet flowers bloom
Petals bend to earth
Grass stretches up.

10. Students will now write a book report. Again, there is a form in the **Appendix.** Use any form that meets your needs. When writing the report, students should focus on the main character and two secondary characters of their choice. They should also write about the reasons for the internment.

    Here are some other things to consider as they are writing. Discuss each one before the writing begins.

    What are the problems for the main character that were carried into adulthood?
    How did the author deal with them and help herself with the problem?
    Finally, have your students put themselves in J.W. Houston's shoes and write about how they would have responded.

    Use the writing/editing format as before. Have students meet with you as many times as necessary to find misspelled words and grammar that needs fixing. When final draft is ready, have students type it out on the computer and print it. Keep all rough drafts and staple to final draft. These will be put on a bulletin board.

11. Another way to enrich your student's vocabulary is to have them use words from the book in sentences. Any form or tense of the word is acceptable. This can be done before or after the book report.

    Here are a few words I chose for my students:

Appalachian	pruned
asserting	quiver
feeble	tirade
ironic	turbulent
permeate	virtue

12. Design a poster representative of the book *Farewell to Manzanar* by J. W. Houston.

When completed, write a caption describing the poster.

13. Display all work on bulletin boards.

Big Boys and Sand Gardens

Here is a story about the previous lesson.

While teaching a unit on World War II and the Japanese Internment Camps, I included an art project where the students created a personal *Japanese Rock/Sand Garden.*

Using shoe boxes as our base, the students poured in sand and then arranged rocks and miniature fake plants. There were plastic forks available to create curved lines in the sand. Students were encouraged to use their creativity and it showed.

Manzanar was an Internment Camp about 200 miles from our school and we learned the Japanese American people interned there created little *Sand Gardens* outside their front doors to give them a sense of comfort and home.

I kept the students' gardens on a high shelf just under the long row of windows in my room. They could go over to their gardens anytime when a non-directed teaching class was in session or if they needed to relax.

One day during nutrition break, there was commotion outside my room and I could see one of my male students involved in a fist-fight with another student. Not wanting him to be suspended for fighting, I rushed out the back door calling to them to, "Stop fighting!"

At the last word, I caught my foot on the root of the large tree shading the patio and down I went.

The two fighters stopped the fight to come over and lift me up. They asked if I was okay. When I answered in the affirmative, they resumed the fight.

Needless to say, both boys were suspended. The day my student returned, I found him at his garden throughout the day using his *Sand Garden* as a way to keep calm.

Never underestimate the power of a craft activity related to the unit to teach powerful lessons, even though the activity might seem juvenile or too young for your students. As I said before about art, it is very impacting on the classroom and on the students. Even students like me, when I was young and felt I wasn't any good at art, found out they enjoyed it and actually created some interesting pieces of art. Give students the opportunity to experience their own creativity and they will find reward in the process.

Lesson 7 / Story: Food, Servants, Lords and Ladies

In this day and age, school principals come into your room for scheduled and surprise visits because of various laws that say, *"This is how we determine your skill as a teacher."* During my career, they were called Stull Evaluations. Although some of those visits were mandated as surprise visits, some of them could be scheduled and I liked inviting administrators in when I knew there was a good lesson in the works. When you involve administration in the life of your classroom, you are in reality helping your students also.

When preparing one of the PBS lessons, I decided serving food was a great idea.

Manor House studies was one of those instances perfect for demonstrating the differences between the social classes and food preparation in England earlier in history.

In one activity, I prepared soup in a large crock pot and brought in my bread machine to make bread. When it was time to eat, *servant* students sat according to their *servant* assignment in the *PBS Manor House*. The more important *servants* sat near the head of the table and the lesser ones sat further away. Role playing was another way to teach my students about the class system of discrimination.

My two aides and I became the servers and the students shared the soup and bread, all the while observing the rule of no talking and keeping heads down while eating.

In contrast, the lesson on food for the wealthy inhabitants was a festive affair. The students and I made name cards for the table, identifying *Lady This* and *Lord That,* as well as a special name card for our own principal who was invited to the luncheon. Students helped with the preparation of finger sandwiches, cookies and hot tea. Everyone washed their hands!

When the principal arrived, students who played the parts of *Lords* and *Ladies* were already seated. The *servant* students were standing by, ready to be of service. Topics for discussion had been practiced prior to our luncheon so there would be no awkward lapses in conversation.

Our principal stayed about 20 minutes, during which time she participated with lively questions and answers to and from students. The food was tasty and everyone who participated learned a bit about the differences between high and low class during that time period in merry old England.

In today's society where students might be allergic to certain foods, check to see if your district prohibits the serving of food. You will have to find another way to be creative with the lesson and I know you will!

Although I did not include the Manor House as a lesson in this book, if you're interested, check out PBS for programs that might inspire your students to write, including

Manor House.

Art work from my lesson is shown below. The students created posters showing the fashion of the day and some of the manors. They also made sweet smelling sachets which were popular at the time, for various reasons. And of course, they wrote about it.

Lesson 8: Greek, Roman and Other Mythologies

Background

Students might have some knowledge regarding Greek, Roman or other mythological heroes because of stories, movies, cartoons and studies. Tell students you are going to challenge them and expand on their knowledge with the following lesson.

Objective

Students will explore the theory of belief systems by studying ancient mythological cultures, including Greek, Roman and other belief systems. They will compare those to their own beliefs and then analyze how their own came to be.

Core Standards

Integration of Knowledge and Ideas.
Key Ideas and Details.
Text Type and Purposes.
Production and Distribution of Writing.
Research to Build and Present Knowledge.

Materials

Find information online to help introduce the topic of mythology.
African, Shoshone Indian Rainbow Myth information available online.
Gods and Goddesses Worksheet within lesson.
Media is available about Greek and Roman mythology. Find one that's appropriate for your students.
Pencils, pens, colored pencils, journals and carbon paper.
Small clay garden pots.
3x5 note cards and metal rings to secure cards together.
Any other materials you deem necessary to help with your lessons.

Instruction

These lessons took about six weeks to complete. Use all or part of them as needed for your students and their understanding of mythology.

1. Find information about Africa, Ancient Greece and the Shoshone Indians regarding how

rainbows came to be. Make copies for students to look at. Read to students and then ask for volunteers to read. At conclusion of reading, ask students to pick one of the rainbow myths to work on.

2. Have students illustrate their chosen myth using colored pencils and a piece of construction paper. Students share their illustration with another person and talk about what it represents. Drawings should be placed in classroom writing folder for posting on bulletin board at end of all lessons.

3. Journal: How do you think these myths developed in ancient cultures? What was their purpose?

4. Give each student the list of gods and goddesses. Have students go over the lists and circle those they might be interested in for further research.

5. Discuss with students the list of gods and goddesses. For example: Why do you think there were so many gods and goddesses? Does knowing what they are responsible for explain any of the beliefs of the time?

6. Journal: Which god or goddess did you choose and why?

7. Students now research in books and online about the god or goddess they chose. Have students take notes and include a list of the sources used. Students make an appointment with the teacher to share their notes and resources.

8. In groups of three or four, students share facts and summaries. Students will then proof read each other's work and make necessary corrections. They now write the information on 3x5 note cards. Students keep all materials and information on their god/goddess in their classroom writing folder for future reference as they complete unit.

9. Journal: What are your family's beliefs?

   All families have some sort of belief system. Tell students the belief could even be an "old-wives-tale" type of belief. For example, a superstition like, *Step on a crack, break your mother's back.*

10. Clay pot craft: Students will use a series of templates gathered from online resources or

books to represent their god or goddess. These will be transferred onto their clay pot. Using carbon paper, or free hand, students transfer illustrations onto pot. This helps students understand the use of pottery and art in everyday life during ancient times.

11. Have students gather all the resources and information they obtained on their god or goddess. They should assemble what they have in chronological order of their research so the writing process can begin.

12. Students should use the format found in **Important Things to Know** and work on their rough draft. The writing should detail their experience studying about myths, gods and goddesses, including their art projects. This also might be a good time to introduce the citing of reference material at the end of their essays. I didn't include information on that process in my notes, but depending on your student's abilities, information can be found online to teach the skill.

13. Students make appointment with teacher to go over their rough draft. Students should read draft aloud to teacher, looking for grammar or spelling mistakes. As before, encourage students to underline or circle words or phrases they aren't sure of. Going over draft a second time, teacher points out areas needing correction. Based on content, teacher encourages students to add more information or expand on a concept in the essay.

14. Students work on drafts as much as needed. When ready, students schedule meeting with the teacher again for final approval. Students type final written draft. Keep all drafts with final typed piece stapled on top. When all students have completed assignment, have them share essays orally with entire class. Post all work on bulletin board with display of note cards, rainbow myth drawings and clay pots placed nearby.

15. Administer Mythology Quiz. Some questions deal with purpose of writing as a review for students. Test and answers are at back of lesson along with picture of student projects.

Greek and Roman Gods and Goddesses

(When there are two listed, the first is Greek, the second, Roman)

- Achilles: A mighty Greek warrior, Hero of Homer's *Iliad*
- Aeneas: Forefather of the Romans, Hero of Virgil's *Aeneid*
- Aphrodite/Venus: Goddess of love and beauty. One of the 12 Olympians. Patroness of lovers, beauty, sometimes of marriage. Considered a war goddess by the Spartans
- Apollo: God of light and purity, music, poetry, prophecy. One of the 12 Olympians. Patron of healers, archers, musicians.
- Ares/Mars: God of wars, also a god of agriculture to the Romans. One of the 12 Olympians, patron of soldiers.
- Artemis/Diana: Goddess of the hunt and moon. One of the 12 Olympians. Patroness of unmarried women, youth and wild animals.
- Atalanta: The swiftest of runners and the best hunter in Ancient Greece
- Athene/Minerva: Goddess of wisdom and handicrafts. Also, of war and agriculture. One of the 12 Olympians
- Bellerophon and Pegasus: A Corinthian hero and the winged horse he tamed
- Castor and Pollux: Twin divinities of the sky. Patrons of athletes and sailors
- Cronus & Rhea/ Saturn & Ops: Rulers of the earth and heavens before Zeus. Parents of six Olympian gods
- Daedalus & Icarus: Inventor and sculptor of Ancient Greece and Icarus, his son
- Demeter/Ceres: Goddess of agriculture. One of 12 Olympians. Patron of farmers
- Deucalion: He and his wife Pyrrha were the only survivors of a great flood
- Dionysus/Bacchus: God of wine. Youngest of the Olympian gods
- Echo & Narcissus: A nymph of the forest. Handsome son of the river god
- The Fates: Three goddesses of destiny. Moirai to the Greeks and Parcae to the Romans
- The Graces: Goddesses of joy and gratitude. Bringers of beauty to young girls
- Hephaestus/Vulcan: God of the forge and master of fire. One of 12 Olympians. Patron of metalworkers and blacksmiths
- Hera/Juno: Queen of the gods. One of 12 Olympians. Protector of married women, childbirth and the home
- Herales/Hercules: Greek hero who achieved divinity when he died. Famous for his 12 labors
- Hermes/Mercury: God of shepherds, travelers, thieves and merchants. One of 12

Olympians

- Hestia/Vesta: Goddess of hearth and home. One of 12 Olympians. Protector of cities and women
- Iris: Goddess of the rainbows. A messenger of the gods
- Janus: God of beginnings. Guardian of passageways
- Jason: Greek hero. Leader of the Argonauts
- Medusa: Beautiful maiden turned into a monster. Was killed by the hero Perseus
- The Muses: Nine goddesses of song, poetry and the arts. Attendants for Apollo
- Niobe: A maiden hurt by boastfulness and pride
- Odysseus/Ulysses: Hero of Homer's *Odyssey*
- Orpheus: Greek musician and poet. One of few mortals to return from underworld
- Pan/Faunus: God of woods, fields and mountains. Patron of shepherds, beekeepers, farmers and hunters
- Pandora: The first woman, who through curiosity, opened a vase or box full of evil
- Persephone/Proserpina: Goddess of the underworld. Bringer of spring
- Poseidon/Neptune: God of the sea. One of 12 Olympians
- Prometheus: A titan who joined forces with Zeus. Founder of the human race and giver of fire
- Pygmalion & Galatea: Sculptor who fell in love with his statue
- Silenus: A woodland deity. Foster father and tutor to Dionysus
- Sisyphus: Condemned to Hades for betraying Zeus
- Tantalus: Mortal king who tried to trick the gods. Condemned to suffer forever in Hades
- Theseus: Legendary king of Athens. Hero who killed the Minotaur
- Zeus/Jupiter: King of the gods. Ruler of the heavens and universe. Disperser of justice and protector of human relations

It's important to go through this list together. There are some words that might need to be defined. For example; *patron*. This is a good language lesson dealing with the gods and goddesses.

Mythology Quiz

Answer the following questions on a separate piece of paper.

1. List the parts of an essay and describe what should be in each part.

2. What is the purpose of journal writing?

3. Why is it important to have many *rough drafts* of an essay?

4. List six Greek gods or goddesses and tell what they were worshiped for.

5. True or false? The Greeks thought the world was flat.

6. Why was it important for the Ancient Greeks to create gods or goddesses?

7. List three facts about the god or goddess you chose. Explain why you selected that one.

8. How many original Olympians were there? List three of them.

9. Describe your Greek clay pot. Give a detailed description of the border and figures.

10. Analyze this unit of study by comparing it to other things you have studied in the past.

Mythology Quiz Answers

1. **Introduction**–What the essay is about
   Thesis–The main idea of the essay
   Body–More information using illustrations and facts with at least three paragraphs
   Conclusion–Wrapping up of information and solidifying facts
   Tell them what you're going to tell them
   Tell them
   Tell them what you told them

2. The purpose of journal writing is to encourage daily writing and sharing of ideas on paper without being punished because of spelling or grammatical mistakes.

3. Each time you do a rough draft, you improve on content, spelling and grammar.

4. Answers will vary.

5. True

6. Answer should be in a complete sentence. Answers may vary but should say something about having their god or goddess protect and look out for them.

7. Answers need to have god or goddess named along with the facts.

8. There were 12. Students need to list three.

9. Answers will vary.

10. Answers will vary.

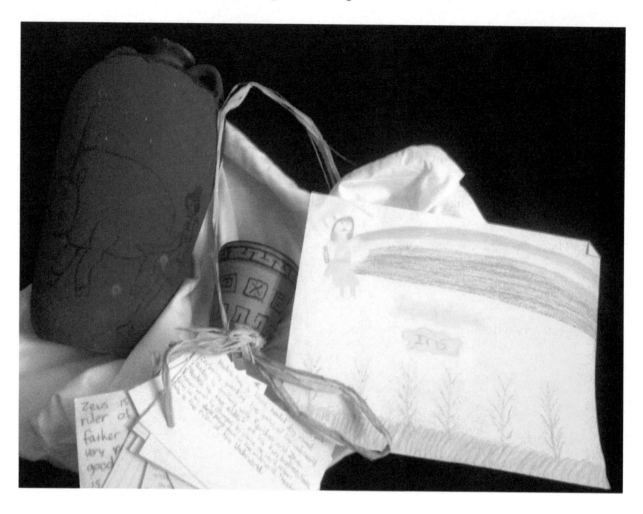

Lesson 9: Eating Healthy vs Fast Food Consumption

Background

Many students today eat fast food as their main source of nutrition. Helping students learn about the dangers of long-term, poor eating habits will allow them to make food choices that may help them stay healthy in years to come.

Objective

Students will explore their eating habits. They will use online resources as part of the lesson. They will learn how to read food labels and strive toward a healthier lifestyle.

Core Standards

Integration of Knowledge and Ideas.
Research to Build and Present Knowledge.
Choosing Language that Expresses Ideas Precisely and Concisely.

Materials

Internet sites dealing with nutrition and food: www.kidshealth.org.
Current books dealing with nutrition.
Media and online programs dealing with nutrition.
Information on Haiku poetry.
Construction paper, magazines, food labels brought from home.
Journal, pens and pencils and any art supplies needed for projects.

Instruction

The following lessons took approximately six weeks.

1. Journal: Make a list of every fast-food establishment you have ever eaten at.

    When students have completed their lists, have them call out the named food places on their list while you list them on the board.

2. In order to elicit interest in the topic of nutrition, show an interesting documentary about eating in fast-food restaurants over a period of time. Find one that shows the deterioration of the body. Have students take notes in journals. As teacher, it is important

to also take notes for future questioning of students prior to watching documentary together. Based on set of questions you provide, divide students into groups with several of those questions. Have each group select a secretary to record answers during group discussion. When groups are finished, each group's secretary presents their feedback to entire class.

3. Homework assignment: Assign students the job of bringing in labels from canned goods and empty chip and cookie bags found in their homes. My students got extra credit for doing this. Once you have a variety of labels, pass them out in class for students to study. They will be looking at fats, cholesterol, sodium, carbohydrates and proteins. Have them define in writing what each category means. They will also look for serving size per container. This is a good small group activity with whole class sharing of information at the conclusion. A good website for discussions is www.kidshealth.org or any other site with that information so students understand the recommended amounts per serving for each item. Food pyramid shown is out of date. Update online.

4. Using old magazines and poster board, have students create a collage demonstrating healthy food on one side and unhealthy food on the other. When completed, they will write on a separate piece of paper describing each section and telling why the food is healthy or not. Students will use prior writing techniques for drafts and rewrites

5. Students will write a final essay talking about the many things studied regarding nutrition. Special focus should be about the benefits healthy eating brings to their lives. Use the writing strategies already learned.

6. For a final fun project, have students select one healthy food with which to do a Haiku poem. A simple formula to use is seven lines:

> First line—one word
> Second line—two words
> Third line—three words
> Fourth line—three words
> Fifth line—two words
> Sixth line—two words
> Seventh line—one word

7. Some of my students used an orange, a pear, a strawberry and a green salad as their food

choice. Creativity counts! Students should get colored paper and cut it out in the shape of their fruit or vegetable. After printing out their poem, attach it to the shape.

Here is a Haiku poem I wrote as an example for students.

Pear
Yellow
Succulent, juicy
Drip, drip, dripping
Down my chin
Love affair
With pear
Yum!

Teacher Notes

Lesson 10: The Love of Animals

Background

Many students have an innate love of animals that transfers into a desire to learn more about them. I picked the study of horses and the book *Seabiscuit, an American Legend* by Laura Hillenbrand. Studying about this particular horse will open doors relating to historical comprehension, analysis and interpretation. Many students feel like underdogs. The horse and main characters in this study often felt that way too.

Objective

Students will research and develop knowledge about the historical nature of the Great Depression and its impact on the people in conjunction with events surrounding the story of the horse, Seabiscuit.

Core Standards

Research to Build and Present Knowledge.
Production and Distribution of Writing.
Integration of Knowledge and Ideas.
Range of Reading.

Materials

If possible, each student should have a copy of the book.
With permission of the school and the parents, show portions of the movie about Seabiscuit from DreamWorks Pictures, 2003.
Tag board, old magazines, journals, computers, printers, pens, pencils and other art supplies as needed.

Instruction

The following lessons took approximately six weeks.

1. Start a discussion about horses with students. Ask if any students have ridden a horse or been to a horse race or if they have seen one on television. Expand discussion to include heroes from other types of sporting events because students will ultimately understand that Seabiscuit was a hero in his own right.

   Journal: Why do we idolize our sports heroes including race horses?

2. Give each student the book if you were able to get enough copies. If not and only able to obtain a few, have students share. There are pictures in the book. Have students look through them. Ask if they know anything about the Great Depression. As teacher, share your own information regarding that time and encourage students to share any info their parents, grandparents, or great-grandparents might have talked about. My information came from grandparents and the grandparents of friends as well as research online.

3. As teacher I approached this unit by reading parts of the book and then showing those same parts of the movie. Have students take notes in their journals during the showing of the movie. Have students share relevant journal entry notes orally during discussions of book and movie.

4. As you discuss the book and movie with students, talk about the main characters; Tom Smith, Charles Howard and Red Pollard. Generate a discussion about each character and their traits.

Here are suggestions from my students taken directly from the board after the discussion:

Tom Smith:
better with animals than people
caring person for horses, and for Red
formal dresser
had limits imposed on his freedom
horse trainer
loner
one of a kind
private person
quiet
reclusive
supportive

Charles Howard:
depressed at times
good salesman
optimistic
people person

risk-taker
self-sufficient
showman
talkative

Red Pollard:
blind in one eye
bulimic
determined
different
fighter
forced to be independent early on
loved books/poetic
often teased
red hair
storyteller
talkative

Based on the characters' attributes from your students' comments or the ones you used from above, have them choose the character they most identify with. Students could also consider Seabiscuit's traits.

5. Students research the character they chose using the book, other books and online resources. Students will write an essay talking about the character as in a biography, using writing format. Toward end of essay, students should discuss why they chose that particular character and why they think they have similar characteristics.

6. Students share essays with a partner for suggestions and rewrites. When finished, students make appointment with you for review, suggestions and further rewrites. Keeping all drafts to staple in back of final draft, student completes the final draft for publication. Have students read their composition aloud to entire class before posting on bulletin board.

7. Students use the outline of a horse's head on tag board to create a collage. I was lucky enough to have an aide who was artistic and drew one for me. Find someone who can do that for you. Based on the character chosen by them, students find pictures in old magazines to represent their character. Example of collage is at end of lesson.

8. Further study and discussion with your class can be done on the topic of being an outsider or underdog. Have students define those terms and give examples of times in their lives when they felt like an outsider or underdog.

9. Journals: What helps overcome the issue of being or feeling like an outsider?
   How did the characters in the story overcome their issues with this topic?
   How did Seabiscuit, with the help of humans, overcome his problems with racing?

Involving the Parents

Julia was a beautiful and bright African American young lady with emotional issues that made regular attendance problematic.

Julia would attend several days and then miss a whole week. When Julia was on her prescribed medication, she had good days, but felt the medication messed with her mind. Many people and students feel this way about medication. I was at a loss trying to figure out how to help her complete her high school education.

One day she mentioned her father was an artist. I asked her to bring in some of his work and she did. He was very skilled and his subject matter was African American heroes as well as African animals.

Right then and there I decided to develop lessons dealing with those men and women he had painted. I had a feeling there could be a great collaboration between Julia's dad and art projects regarding his subject matter. I could also craft lessons about the Civil Rights Movement and incorporate writing.

The subject matter of African American History and the Civil Rights Movement gave me many different topics from which to choose.

With Julia's permission, I called her dad and asked if he would come to class and give the students a lesson on his painting technique and style. He was quite willing to do anything to keep his daughter attending school.

Julia helped me design a bulletin board displaying her dad's work and another board to show our students' written and art work when we had completed our studies.

It wasn't all smooth sailing, but it was the start of better attendance and with the added help of the school psychologist and weekly counseling sessions, she began to attend more regularly. Involving her dad in the educational process was the key that kept Julia in school so she was able to graduate.

The last week of school she brought me a gift. It was a beautiful daisy pin that had belonged to her grandmother. It turned out both our grandmothers had been named Daisy.

On graduation day, I gave Julia one of my grandma's daisy pins.

Teacher Notes

Lesson 11: African American History and The Civil Rights Movement

Background

It's important in this day and age for students to understand the history of racism and prejudice. We live in a multicultural society and need to understand that hopefully, we are more alike than different. Understanding each other's differences can often encourage compassion and empathy. Utilizing the talents of the father of one of my students, I was able to keep the student in school and introduce the father as an artist who painted Africa American heroes and African animals.

Objective

Students will investigate African American history. They will also explore their own feelings about the Civil Rights Movement, prejudice and racism by studying art, literature and events during the Civil Rights Movement.

Core Standards

Integration of Knowledge and Ideas.
Research to Build and Present Knowledge.
Craft and Structure.
Choosing Language that Expresses Ideas Precisely and Concisely.
Reading Standards for Literary Nonfiction include: Functional text in the form of personal essays, biographies and memoirs.

Materials

Journals, pens, pencils, colored pencils, colored markers, craft paper, poster board, empty oatmeal cereal containers, foam craft boards, fabric, faux leather and non-toxic tempera paint.
Documentaries that show events that happened during the Civil Rights Movement.
Books dealing with the history of African Americans.
Books that showcase the writings of African American writers.
Online resources.

Instruction

The following lessons took approximately six weeks.

Unlocking the Writing Process

1. Find books or online resources with the writings of Langston Hughes and Maya Angelou. There are several poems that would be appropriate–your choice. Have students read the poems and then have a discussion about style and the meaning of words. Similes and the metaphors in the poetry will be discussed.

2. Journal: What are the feelings you experienced from the poetry and stories you just read? Students should compare the different styles of writing of both authors in an oral class discussion.

3. Journal: Write a poem or short story in the style of Langston Hughes or Maya Angelou expressing or talking about something that happened to you.

4. Using the writing and correcting technique from prior lessons, have students share their draft from above journal with another student, looking for ways to improve their writing. When student is ready, schedule an appointment with you for further correction and drafts leading to final paper.

5. Journal: What is your definition of prejudice? Give an example of prejudice at your school or in your neighborhood.

6. Having an artistic father who was willing to demonstrate his style of art to students was a great gift. His technique utilized the outlining of a subject with bold colors, then filling in the background, almost like a film negative. Find a person to demonstrate their artistic style to your students.

7. If that resource is not available, research artists and their techniques so students can replicate the style of art. In my class, students observed the painting technique and asked questions of the artist. Have students trace outline from photo copies of African American heroes or draw their own picture. Using bold colors, students fill in their artwork as demonstrated by the artist.

8. Students research the hero they drew. Have them take notes in their journal for later reference. In pairs, students share artwork and information gathered. Have students write a short biography of the hero they used for their art. Correct draft as before and when ready, post on bulletin board. My students mainly used Langston Hughes, Frederick Douglass and Maya Angelou.

9. Students use a dye cut technique to design additional artwork representative of African art, featuring animals from Africa. Have students go online or look in books furnished by you, to find an animal. Using a foam craft board about 6 inches in diameter, have students trace the animal so they can transfer the tracing onto the foam board. Pressing firmly, transfer drawing into foam board. See picture at end of lesson.

10. Using washable, black tempera paint, have students paint over the now indented drawing of their animal. While paint is still wet, students turn painting over and press onto white craft paper. Students carefully remove foam painted board and let both board and paper dry. This is a dye cut technique and both board and craft paper will be used to create a bulletin board along with the African American hero they painted.

11. Look for resources that show *The Children's March* that happened in Birmingham, Alabama in 1963. It is a story of young people who braved fire hoses and police dogs. Their protest/march, as well as other events, encouraged President Johnson to introduce the Civil Rights Act of 1964. The main focus of the story helps students understand the power of political movements and how they can make a difference. Equality, historical perspective and their own political agendas are explored.

12. After exploring the emotionally powerful subject of *The Children's March*, have another art/craft project. I chose the making of a drum called **Baby Brekete Drum,** used by the Ashanti of Ghana. Brekete are Ghana's version of the Nigerian jun-jun drums and played on festive occasions by being held in the armpit.

13. Have students bring in empty oatmeal containers–the tall, circular kind. Students now cover the cylinder with fabric and glue it in place. Use the faux leather to cover the top and bottom of the "drum" and have students create decorative straps. Listen to authentic drumming from Africa using online resources. Have a drumming concert with your class.

14. For the final project, have students explore the current racial issues present in the world today and create a collage to show those problems. On a separate piece of paper, students should write a description of their collage and suggest possible ways to solve the problem of racial inequality. If possible, bring in guest speakers from the community to share their personal stories with the students.

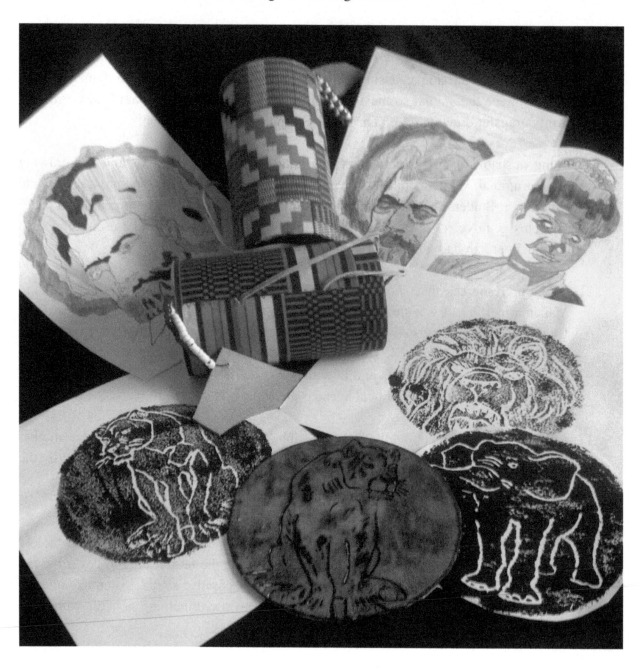

Lesson 12: Part I–How We View the World

Background

Students with special needs tend to put themselves down and not value their contributions to friends, family, school and society. By reading the book, *the curious incident of the dog in the night-time* by Mark Haddon, and studying other well-known people with disabilities, perhaps students can understand their problems and difficulties make them strong, unique and define who they are.

Objective

To show students they don't have to be famous to be successful.

Through this two-part study of famous people and fictional characters who have difficulties, students will learn they can turn problems into assets.

Core Standards

Integration of Knowledge and Ideas.

Research to Build and Present Knowledge.

Choosing Language that Expresses Ideas Precisely and Concisely.

Materials

A copy of the above book for each student. Students can also share, or it can just be read aloud by the teacher.

Materials found online for Helen Keller, and Ansel Adams.

Journals, pens, pencils, poster/tag board, personal phone or camera.

Access to computers and printers.

Post-it notes.

Assignment sheet at end of Part I–description of pictures to be taken.

Instruction

The following lesson took approximately six weeks.

1. Introduce the book, *the curious incident of the dog in the night-time,* which is about a boy named Christopher Boone who has Autism. Autism is a disorder that begins in childhood and is often characterized by marked deficits in communication, social interaction, preoccupation, and restrictive or repetitive behavior patterns.

2. Journal: Students should write about someone they might know who has Autism. If they

don't know anyone with autism, have them write about someone with a difficult problem.

3. If you have copies of the book for all students, start reading the book aloud as students follow along. Students use Post-it notes to mark in the parts of the book they want to discuss or refer back to later. Ask for student volunteers to also read aloud. Continue reading the book each day as you go on with the next parts of **How We View the World.**

4. Introduce students to Helen Keller. She was born in 1887 and at almost two years of age became sick and lost her vision and hearing. Find information and documentaries to tell her story of overcoming these disabilities with the help of Anne Sullivan, who was also partially blind. Students should take notes and keep them in their writing notebooks.

5. Journal: Imagine you have a friend who is blind, but can still hear. You are taking them to an amusement park. Describe in detail all the things they are hearing and smelling.

6. As you continue reading the book from the beginning of the lesson, take time to discuss various aspects of the dilemmas faced by the main character, Christopher Boone. I read the book before introducing it to my students and took notes so I would have discussion questions ready as well as talking about what the students brought up.

7. Introduce Ansel Adams who was born in 1902. Adams was homeschooled and became a famous photographer and conservationist. Find information and documentaries to tell his story of working with his Attention Deficit Disorder and the sharing of his beautiful photos of nature. Again, students should take notes and keep them in their writing notebooks.

8. Journal: We all have times when we are unable to focus. What do you do to help yourself when you can't focus? Share different strategies you use when you are restless.

9. As students complete the book and the research about Helen Keller, Ansel Adams, and our fictional character Christopher Boone, introduce the assignment from the worksheet at end of lesson.

Note: The phone/camera technology we use today wasn't available when I did the lesson. Students used disposable cameras. Students should use their own phone or a loner camera. Help students upload photos to be printed. Hard copies are needed to complete assignment.

10. Once the pictures are available, students will do a layout on firm poster board. Have students label each section; their name from their viewpoint, and then from the viewpoint of Helen Keller, Ansel Adams and Christopher Boone. The result will be a photo collage of sorts. Example of art project at end of this lesson. Students complete writing assignment as detailed on worksheet.

Worksheet: How We View the World

By studying Christopher Boone, Helen Keller and Ansel Adams, we have seen how they view the world. You will now see how you view the world through the pictures you take.

Christopher Boone: An autistic 15-year-old boy

Helen Keller: A blind and deaf woman who learns to communicate by touch and braille

Ansel Adams: A man who became famous for his black and white photography. He had ADHD–Attention Deficit Disorder with Hyperactivity.

Your turn: What is your story? What is your viewpoint on the world?

Your assignment: Use your own phone to take black and white and color pictures. You have a week to take pictures.

Five of the pictures should be from the viewpoint of Christopher Boone
Five of the pictures should be from the view point of Helen Keller
Five should be from the viewpoint of Ansel Adams

The remaining pictures can tell your story or viewpoint.
Remember to take pictures that have contrast–strong darks and lights
Remember also to use appropriate subject matter–no inappropriate pictures.
The pictures will be uploaded.

When all are printed, you will create a photo layout on posterboard telling their stories and your story in pictures. You will then create a written description of your photo board using the writing techniques from previous assignments. When ready with your first draft, make an appointment to go over your written work. When all corrections and rewrites are completed, type out your work and print it. It will be attached to your collage and posted on the bulletin board.

Teacher Notes

Lesson 12: Part II–How We View the World

Background

Students who require extra support receive specialized academic instruction. When I was teaching, the program was called Resource Specialist Program—RSP. There is a stigma attached to being labeled and students have had to deal with this most of their school careers. Some students call RSP *really stupid people* or *really stupid program*, which of course, isn't true. It breaks my heart and makes me sad.

There are other programs available for students with more significant needs like SDC–Special Day Class and other programs for other issues. Your student can be helped!

My point is, the sooner students accept who they are and where their talents lie, as well as what can be done to remediate their issues, the more they can progress as human beings. Isn't this true of all of us and our strengths and issues? Part II puts those problems and stigmas out there for students to deal with right now.

By this time in my class, most students were ready to face their disability. This is a sensitive, but important topic because some students feel they don't have value.

Objective

To show students what they think makes them "less than," can actually become a strength. By reading a book about their learning disability, students can come to understand what it is and ways to work around and with the disability.

Core Standards

Integration of Knowledge and Ideas.
Research to Build and Present Knowledge.
Choosing Language that Expresses Ideas Precisely and Concisely.

Materials

Find books online that deal with different kinds of disabilities.
I chose a series that was appropriate for students in my class. Choose for yours.
Computer access for your students to research their particular issue.
Worksheet: **How We "See" the World.**
Pencils, pens, writing journal, writing folder.
Computer, printer for final writing project.

Instruction

These lessons will take approximately three to four weeks.

1. Journal: You are in special education because you need some extra help. What are you getting help with? (If students are in denial and not wanting to acknowledge their difficulty, have them write about school subjects that are difficult for them.)

2. Do some research about people with known learning, emotional and physical disabilities. Have a class discussion about people with disabilities and introduce the people you found. Remind them of the subjects from Part I of this study. Do the students know any others? List people and their disabilities on the board. Talk about the accomplishments of the listed people as well as their struggles.

3. Journal: How do you think the above people overcame or learned to work with their disability?

4. Give students the worksheet **How We "See" the World** at the end of this lesson. This is a review of Helen Keller, Christopher Boone and Ansel Adams. It also places the student in the mix. This worksheet deals with the topics of:

   Entertainment
   Favorite Colors
   Hobbies
   Hopes/Dreams
   Jobs
   Learning styles
   Legacy
   Pets

   There are other topics too. It helps the student see and hopefully understand how disabilities do not have to determine success and their place in the world.

5. Using the books you chose about your students' disabilities, find a way to introduce them. The way I did it was to lay the books out on a large table and have them go and chose one. Interestingly enough, most students chose the book that was closest to their own disability, which is of course what I wanted! Students now read the book and take notes as they read.

6. Using book report form in back of book or any form you like, have students complete their book report. As before, meet with them as they complete first rough draft and subsequent drafts until ready for final draft.

7. When all book reports are completed, have students share their reports with the entire class. This may be difficult for some of the students, but impress upon them how important it is for sharing about their disability because it helps by educating the other students about different disabilities. This, in turn, hopefully allows for acceptance.

8. For the final essay, students will write about all the things they have studied in Parts I and II. It could be organized by starting with their disability and then discussing other disabilities and what they learned from the study.

9. Finally, have students report on whether studying about their own disability helped them understand themselves better. Did it give them hope?

Again, go through the prior writing process where students meet with you as they write each draft. Final draft should be typed out. Include all rough drafts behind final draft. Doing this step shows the progress the student has made in his/her writing. It's visual. Post all work including worksheet on how they see the world on bulletin boards. If a bookcase or shelf is available near bulletin board, place the books they used nearby.

How We "See" The World

Categories	Your Name	Helen Keller	Chris Boone	Ansel Adams
Learning Styles				
Hobbies				
Type of Books Read				
Job				
Pets				
Favorite Toy				
Entertainment				
Pessimist/ Optimist				
Favorite Food				
Favorite Color				
Family Members				
Difficulties Faced				
Hopes/Dreams				
Contributions/Legacy				

More Teacher Stories

It Was a Start

I remember setting up my first classroom, then standing at the door looking in at what I had created and thinking: Wonderful things are going to happen here!

Many wonderful things did happen in that 1st grade classroom and then in the 4th grade the following year; but some mistakes occurred too.

When teaching 4th grade, I loved having the students experience the wonder of growing things and I set up a small garden area on the back patio where the students planted seeds and watched them enter the world and grow.

I had one very large pot where I planted some geranium seeds. It was the best geranium plant I've ever had! This lovely area was also my time-out space for the students who needed a bit of thinking time.

Ryan needed some thinking time one day just before lunch. He had been using some very adult language and was not responding to directions to cease and desist, so therefore, time-out.

The desk where Ryan went to sit until he could be appropriate was next to the beautiful, large geranium plant. Down he sat and I went back inside to finish the lesson.

I'm embarrassed to continue on with this story, but hoping it will help a beginning teacher to move past his or her mistakes and become a better teacher.

When we got back from lunch and I was looking around the room, Ryan's desk was empty. Where was Ryan?

Yes, Ryan was still on the patio where I had told him to stay. Rushing to the back door I saw that Ryan had fallen asleep at the desk and hadn't realized we had gone to lunch. I was mortified at what had happened.

Making sure Ryan was okay, I sent for a late lunch and apologized for leaving him there. Fortunately, I was not fired for my mistake.

You will make mistakes in your teaching career. It's a given. The important thing is to learn from them and become a better teacher because of the experience. I certainly did!

The Boy, the Desk, the Gun

Having first taught for three years at the private elementary school near my home, I decided to branch out and applied to Los Angeles Unified School District. My family needed more income and my daughter needed braces so dental insurance was an incentive.

I had a friend who was a principal at a local soon-to-be middle school in the San Fernando Valley and wanted to hire me to teach 6th grade. I was excited until one morning the headlines in the newspaper said, "**All New Hires to LAUSD Mandated to Inner City.**" It was 7:00 in the morning when I called the principal.

His response to my question was, "I can't hire you now."

I interviewed at three different elementary schools and they all wanted me. I think I chose the wrong one, but I learned much about myself and about teaching during that year, so it probably was the right one after all.

The first thing I learned was the teachers from the previous year who taught 4th grade had thoughtfully organized the students into four classes for the new 5th grade year. But the current 5th grade teachers had reorganized the students and placed all the difficult ones into the classrooms of myself and another new teacher–they obviously didn't want the difficult students.

Hmmm, I guess I was learning about survival now–the survival of teachers already there wanting a stress-free year.

The second thing I learned was even though I spoke English and the students spoke English, our dialect was different. I found this out the first day of school when I was supposed to read the names of last year's 5th graders who were temporarily in my room. I was tasked with telling them their new room assignments for sixth grade–blank stares. I asked them to tell me their names–I couldn't understand them either. The solution was to walk around the room and show them the list so they could find their names and see which room they were assigned to–just in time, as the 15 minutes allotted for this was up.

One of the things I loved doing in each and every classroom where I taught was arranging the room to achieve the best learning environment for the students and after a few rearrangements in my inner-city classroom, settled on a U-shaped design. By the way, it didn't take much time for the students to understand me, and me them.

One day during a math lesson, as I was walking around the inside of the U helping students, one of the boys whispered, "Herman is pointing a gun at your back."

I nodded that I had heard him but continued around the class helping with the lesson. I then walked to the outside of the U and when I got to Herman's desk, leaned over and reached into it. He immediately put his hand to the front of his jacket and I knew I had found the gun. I took it from him whereby he screamed at me, picked up his desk and threw it across the room. He was an angry boy who felt powerless. Having a gun made him feel powerful. Herman had been present when a friend was shot and killed.

Sending a cooperative student to get some help, the situation was finally under control. Because this was before weapons were a reason for expulsion, Herman was "expelled" from my room and traded for another student, Evan, who wasn't doing well in his class. I was relieved. Herman did better in the new class and so did Evan in my class.

Most of the new teachers hired that year quit at Thanksgiving. A few of us stayed and I'm glad I did, but knew if I stayed past that year, I would give up on teaching. Most days I cried all the way home and toward the end of the school year began applying to other districts.

Fortunately, I was hired to teach Special Education for Burbank Unified. At night and during summer vacations I continued my education at California State University, Northridge and got several more teaching credentials and certificates.

The reality is I became a better teacher because of my experiences in inner city. In your career and journey as teachers you will have your own events that test you and your abilities. Trust your instincts and seek help with the things you aren't sure of. Many other seasoned professionals want to help–that's why they became teachers. Let them give you advice. You will do the same when you are the seasoned one. I know because I did.

I became a mentor teacher when I taught 4th grade in another state. It was rewarding to be able to help a beginning teacher. And, then at the high school level, I worked for several years as a support provider and consulting teacher. I didn't always know the answers, but I knew how to direct the teacher to the right resources. I believe we want to be the best we can be to help our students succeed.

Field Trips and other Stories

Another story from inner-city; I was told to keep my two classroom doors locked and when someone knocked, open the opposite door. The sight of masses of students running to the fences and climbing them when police showed up on campus during recess was also surprising. No one wanted to get caught for truancy or other things.

Gang rivalry was strongly felt at my elementary school and one had to be careful about the colors worn on clothing. One day I was wearing a neutral color–white, on my suit jacket. I was finishing a science lesson where we had planted seeds in cups. The students placed the finished product on bookshelves under the row of windows. One student, angry at the world and me, picked up his seed cup and threw it. All the wonderful, moist dirt landed on my gang neutral, white jacket.

At the time, I had a temporary teacher's aide and he managed to subdue the student and take him to the office. My jacket was never the same. Years later I heard my former student had joined a gang. He died in a gang fight. So sad to hear someone with such potential never got to use it. I believe he could have become a professional athlete in any number of sports.

At Christmas that year, I brought gifts to give the students before they headed home for the holiday break. Most of my students had been at school, but a few weren't there that day so I decided to drive the gifts to their homes before I headed home. Getting lost a few times, I finally had delivered all but one gift. I found the young man's house but he wasn't there. Jonathan was his name.

Jonathan was one of my favorite students as he was the first one to defend me and tell the other students to, "Be quiet and listen to Mrs. Forletta!" He must have been a leader because the students did what he said.

Jonathan's grandmother was at home and that's how I learned he was being raised by her in great squalor. She was stoned and could barely talk. I learned a little more that day about the sad conditions some of my students lived in. It opened my eyes and heart to doing all I could to help them succeed and improve the situations they and their families lived in through education.

Later in the year when students trusted me more, they shared how when gunfire erupted in their neighborhoods, especially at night, their mothers and grandmothers would lay on top of the young ones to protect them from bullets.

Changing topics; let's talk about counting. We teachers know how to count! We count our students when on busses, in line and when back on busses after field trips. One field trip to the Hollywood Bowl where there were hundreds and hundreds of students and many, many busses to load into after the performance, found me one student short.

Oh, no!! I had lost one of my students.

One of my sweet girls was missing and the busses had to leave in the order they drove in so the busses behind them could also leave. I only had minutes before we had to go. It had been about five minutes so far when Jocelyne showed up! She had actually been listening to me when I pointed out landmarks to follow to get back to the bus. Thank goodness for students who listen. I know that was the only time in my 30-year career that I temporally lost a student! Oh, I mean besides Harry who fell asleep near the geranium plant.

A few weeks before my school year was over, I was lucky enough to take a week-long field trip with most of my students to a camp in the local mountains where they could learn about nature. It was a wonderful experience for all of us. We had bonded during the year and this was a gift. The students, many who had never been away from home, learned much and I learned how much I would miss them.

That was always the hard part–letting them go after a year together. I'm pretty sure this has happened to you too. When you spend a year with a class, getting to know them, teaching them, settling into a comfortable routine and then having to say, "Good-bye" is so upsetting.

I finally, after several years of teaching, came to terms with this part of the job. I learned to appreciate what it had been and look forward to a new school year and new students to bond with.

Sometimes it's necessary and okay to say, "Good-bye!"

Paying Attention

One of the things I observed while teaching in inner city was the way students, especially boys, acted tough in order to intimidate others. An example is when a possible fist fight might take place. Rather than actually fight, the boys come face to face and chest to chest without ever touching. Moving side to side and saying braggadocio phrases, they try and intimidate the other one. One of them usually backs down and the one who didn't is the winner.

The reason I bring this up is to explain how I became the winner the first week I started teaching Special Education classes for students with learning disabilities at a junior high school. One of my students was a boy in 9th grade and quite tall for his age–much taller than I was at 5'5". He was mouthing off in class where I was trying to conduct a small group reading lesson. When repeated suggestions to stop went unheeded, I asked him to step outside the class into the hallway so we could talk.

I was quiet and calm when I told him his behavior was unacceptable. Then I did like the boys in inner city and repeated my demands for cooperation. He was quite surprised but agreed to comply with the class rules. Now, the important part; when we went back into the class, he strolled in all macho man, like he had won the argument. The only thing was, the transom window above the door was open, so the students heard the entire conversation and knew who succeeded. I didn't have trouble with him or most of the other students in that class after that episode. I believe in today's world I would not be able to challenge a student that way, but it worked.

Another thing happened at the school that taught me a lesson in taking a step back when emotions became too strong. One of my girl students had a difficult home life. I was aware of some of the issues but not all of them. Stella was petite with beautiful long, whitish, blond hair. One day she came to school and all her hair had been chopped down to about two inches around her head. She had done it herself in retaliation to something that happened at home and that's when I found out about the rest of the difficult things she had been dealing with.

I wanted to adopt her then and there. Meeting with my principal and telling her my plan, she spoke about more reasonable ways to help this girl which we did implement. Getting too emotionally involved wouldn't have helped this student and I learned to take a step back.

Along those lines, a counselor at the school gave me some sound advice when I was in his office crying and bemoaning the fact I couldn't get through to a particular student.

He told me, "You've done everything you can and you set the stage for the next teacher to possibly be the one to get through to him, so you have to let it go and focus on the students you can help."

So, the lesson for teachers is to pay attention to how students deal with their issues because you might be able to use the very same technique to help them. It's worth a try. It worked for me. Also, getting emotionally involved may work sometimes, but most times gets in the way of doing the right thing for that student and all your other students.

Hang in there. You can accomplish what you need to do in order to help them. Take time off if need be. The vice principal at the inner-city school told me one day when I was in his office and having a difficult time controlling my tears, "Take a day off when you feel like this. You have ten sick days. Use them when you need to take a step back. You will be a far more effective teacher."

I listened to him and made it through the school year. I used all ten sick days!

Climbing the Walls

Climbing the walls sounded like a good title, but I really mean *Climbing the Shelves*. The student I'm talking about would have liked to climb the walls if he had had Velcro on his fingers. Since he didn't, he climbed the book shelves in my classroom.

Ronald was a student in my RSP junior high class. As I've said earlier, RSP stands for Resource Specialist Program where student's receive special help if they have a learning disability, behavior and or emotional issues, to name a few reasons. Ronald had a combination of issues. He was a good-looking young man and much taller than most 7th grade boys. He also had an abundance of energy. I had placed his desk at the front of my classroom in hopes his attention could be held by my brilliant oration–just kidding–I just wanted to get through to him on any given day and if he was in the front of the class, my chances of doing that were better.

We were doing a history lesson on this day and I was walking up and down the center aisle as I gave volunteers the opportunity to read aloud. All of a sudden there was muted laughter from the class and all eyes were on the front of the room.

On either side of the chalkboard were floor to ceiling bookcases securely attached to the wall and Ronald had made a dash to the right side of the chalkboard and up to the top of that bookcase where he sat with a big grin on his face. I had to laugh at the scene in front of me which gave the class permission to unmute their laughter.

What to do? If I told Ronald to get down, would he? He had ODD, which is Oppositional Defiance Disorder and he would, of course, do the opposite of what I asked of him.

So, I just stood there and said, "It appears that Ronald must have something very important to tell us! Ronald, the floor, or rather the bookshelf is yours. Go for it!"

He thought for a moment and then got down. We continued on with our lesson.

Another time during a reading lesson I moved the small group I was working with outside to the little patio by the door. It was a lovely day and nice to be outside. There were six students with their chairs, sitting in a circle. They took turns reading and as we were discussing the theme of the story, James leaned on the legs of his chair so he was tipped slightly backwards. A rather large knife fell out of his pocket and he grabbed it just before it hit the ground. I didn't say a thing and the lesson continued on to the end. As we finished up, I asked James to wait for a second and when it was just the two of us, I held out my hand. He then knew I had seen the knife and he handed it to me.

James had been in fear of another student and brought the knife to protect himself. I got another teacher to cover my class and James and I walked to the principal's office.

At this point in my career, when you brought a weapon to school, there were consequences, unlike years earlier in inner-city.

James wasn't expelled, rather transferred to another school because he was in Special Education. A regular education student would have been expelled. I wish I could have continued to work with him as he was a nice kid–he just made the wrong decision.

As teachers, we don't always know what the day will bring. We hope for smooth days but are ready for the climbers and knife bringers. We hope ultimately our students are learning and enjoying the process. At least I always hoped that would happen. But we prepare for the days when things don't go smoothly, until it becomes second nature to react to each situation automatically, in ways that will ensure our students safety and the learning environment of our classrooms.

Joys and Challenges

Teaching in a mountain community, Incline Village, Nevada, had its share of joys and challenges. One of the joys was the beautiful scenery, along with the changing of the seasons. Although I was born in Pennsylvania, I grew up in Southern California where our seasonal changes are subtle, so experiencing the beauty was like three dimension and surround sound compared to black and white.

My first winter and first big snow storm brought huge challenges. For example, snow days. If the snow storm was dangerous, a snow day was called and I was supposed to get a phone call telling me to stay home. There was a phone chain and then I was to call the next teacher on the list and so on until all the teachers and staff were notified.

One day I woke up to a big storm and was sure I would be called, but no call came, so I got into my car and off I went. I drove down treacherous mountain roads to school. I barely got there only to find the parking lot empty except for deep drifts of snow. I thought, is this what the school does to new teachers–see if they are up to the challenges of mountain living? A parent arrived shortly after I did and needed to get into one of the classrooms to save the class pet–a Guinea Pig, and take it home so it wouldn't freeze, therefore my trip was worthwhile. I helped save a Guinea Pig!

When I got home, I called the teacher who was supposed to call me. She was embarrassed and said she forgot about me being new and had just called the teacher on her list from the year before. Two days later when school reopened, she brought me a box of candy to apologize. It was delicious!

One of my students that first year in the 2nd grade classroom was a beautiful little boy who had been adopted and because I had experience as a Special Education Teacher, his mom requested me. Why? He had fetal alcohol syndrome. His birth mother was an alcoholic and continued to drink while pregnant.

Ricky would fly into angry rages in the classroom and start tearing down bulletin boards and destroying anything in his path. Although there are many ways this syndrome presents itself, in Ricky's case behavioral issues and learning difficulties were the main problems.

The most worrisome thing that happened with him was on a bus trip when he tried to jump out of the window of the bus while on a freeway headed home from a field trip. I had already given a heads-up to a fellow teacher asking for help if he started to spiral. I was seated by the window and he was next to me on the seat when all of a sudden, he flung himself toward the partially opened window. I grabbed him and was able to secure his arms cross-chest, which was a safe way to hold him so he wouldn't harm himself or others.

The problem continued however because he was kicking out and trying to get away. My teacher friend sitting across the aisle managed to hold his legs down. It was a long two-hour trip home and we were both exhausted, but he was safe and so were the other children.

Ricky had good moments throughout the school year but his problems continued as he progressed through the grades. It wasn't his fault he had been burdened with this problem and everyone continued to try and help him manage his rages, including the family that loved him.

Here's my advice to you, form bonds with fellow teachers. I always volunteered for the Social Committee so I could interact with all the teachers and get to know everyone. It's a wonderful thing when they have your back and you have theirs. You become a family and it's better when you get along and support one another. The school year is much more enjoyable too. And in the case with Ricky, my friend and fellow teacher gave much needed support when I needed it.

Ninja Stars and Holiday Programs

Many things happened in 2nd grade the two years I taught it. I was living in the beautiful community I've talked about before. There was the time one of my boys was throwing a Ninja Star at trees before school. I saw what he was doing as I arrived and retrieved it from him. Hurrying to set up my class, I shoved it in my purse and forgot about it. Later that day when I went to pick my husband up from the airport in the days when you could still meet the plane, I went through security and was stopped for having a weapon in my purse.

I laughed and said, "I don't have a weapon in my purse."

The security guard showed me the x-ray and said, "That's a weapon!"

When I told him I had taken it from a 2nd grade student earlier in the day, I'm not sure he believed me. I had to pick it up on the way out. His mom laughed and fell off the little chair in my room during our parent conference. The Ninja Star incident was my first order of business for the conference. She got it back that day.

And then, there were the more serious and life changing, emotional situations that happened. I had a little girl, Karen, in my class one of those years. She was a sweet, pretty little student and very shy. At her parent conference meeting, her mother was having a difficult time staying on the small chair. She reeked of alcohol and it was evident she was going to lose her lunch. I rushed to bring the trash can to her as she vomited into it. She apologized and expressed her desire to go to rehabilitation. She said, "I'm looking into it." I let the school psychologist know what was going on with Karen and her mom.

Our Christmas program came a few weeks later and our whole school convened on a stormy, snowy night at the local junior high where the auditorium could accommodate us. My class performed well and after all the performances were completed and we were having refreshments, Karen's mother came up to me to say hello. She was drunk, so drunk I didn't think it was safe for her to drive Karen home. I offered to take Karen home in my car while the mom followed me. We all made it without incident. She then asked me to call a rehab for her and I did.

All the arrangements were made, which took quite a while, when at the last minute, she decided not to go.

I called a neighbor to come and stay with them that night and soon after, they moved away. I don't know what happened to that sweet girl and her mom, but I hope they eventually got the help they needed.

I think I became too involved in this case, but I did what I thought was right. Again, I let the psychologist and school administrator know what had happened.

Always, always let the principal, psychologist or another administrator know what is going on with your students in situations like I've described so help can be obtained. The point of being a teacher and being responsible for your students also means everyone else at the school is part of the team. Teams work together for the best outcome. The student's safety and success are the goal. Use all the tools available to you to help your students.

Unusual Teaching Styles

Sammy was a 2nd grade student in my class. It was the beginning of school and I was getting to know each of my students. Sammy and I had not started out very well as he was constantly interrupting the class. I was using everything I had been taught in methodology classes to get him on track. Nothing was working.

One day near recess, I was tired. I had moved his desk to the front of the class. I had also given him the responsibility of class helper and he had passed out papers for me. Now he was at his desk using a ruler to tap out a rhythm on the top of that very desk. I told him if he didn't stop, he would lose the right to go out to recess, which meant I would also lose my recess. The tapping continued and when the bell rang, both Sammy and I stayed inside.

I brought his desk right up to my desk and as I sat down, I put some papers I needed to grade in front of me. Using my right hand to mark on the papers, I picked up a ruler with my left and began tap, tap, tapping on my desk top. He continued his tapping. I didn't look at Sammy. This went on for about two minutes when I noticed out of the corner of my eye a slight smile on his face.

Finally, an opening; I looked up at him and smiling said, "Kind of silly, aren't we?"

He agreed and we both stopped tapping. Sammy needed attention obviously and during that recess, I gave it to him. We talked about him and his family and got to know each other a little bit. I'm not saying the problem evaporated that very day, but Sammy was much more compliant with directions from that point on.

Gary was another student at the same school in a different year. I was now teaching 4th grade, which turned out to be my favorite elementary grade. Gary was also an attention seeker and would go out of his way to distract any and all the other students in the class. He did this in many ways, but his favorite distraction was to make faces; and wow could he make faces! Scary!

I had worked with all my other students to ignore Gary and carry on, and they did. Now Gary wasn't getting the attention he so wanted so I thought about another way to give him the attention he needed. It was important to solve this problem; for him focus enough to do the school work now and in the future.

I tried many of the same techniques I had used with Sammy, but to no avail. No, I didn't make faces!

One evening at home, an idea came to me–maybe if he could see how he looked when he made those faces, he would stop. It was worth a try.

I called him up to my desk the next morning and said, "You can make faces anytime you want but you need to sit at my desk when you do."

He thought that was great and a short time later, walked to my desk, sat down and started to make grotesque faces. The thing was, I had placed a small mirror on the desk so he immediately would see himself. That's all it took. That particular behavior stopped! He focused more regularly on his school work most days. I gave him jobs in the classroom so he felt he was important in his ability to help. His parents also worked on those improved behaviors at home and he seemed a calmer and happier young boy.

Methodologies are great and I used the ones I was taught, but the most successful ones came from "*ah ha*" moments I had when trying to figure out how to help the more challenging student behaviors! The behavioral tools you have in your tool box will come in handy some days. Other days, try something new and see if it works.

Students and Their Babies

The high school I taught at was special in many ways. In one way, it had the best and most diversified group of staff and teachers than any other school I taught at. No two of us were alike and yet we worked and taught together like a well-oiled machine. We had a "Buddy-System" where each teacher worked with a group of students. The students would choose their own teacher buddy based on personality, classes they were taking, and whatever else they deemed important to get the extra help they needed. The student could meet with the teacher anytime they felt they needed help and it worked. Most students who had come from the traditional high schools and wanted to get back there after making up credits ended up staying at our school mainly because of all the support they received.

Another way our school was special was the teen pregnancy program and baby/toddler nursery on site. The pregnant teens were required to take parenting classes prior to the birth of their babies and then work in the nursery after their baby was born. The women in charge of the nursery were credentialed and excellent teachers, so that the new moms learned how to parent.

Several of my students were parents through the years. For most of them, having a child gave them the incentive to work hard and complete their education so they could take care of and support their family.

Speaking of support, my program, RSP, worked with a state funded program where the students could get job training and job experience while getting paid and then being able to put that experience on their resume. It was a win-win situation. The students didn't always like the job they had, but I told them, "Welcome to the real world," and, "That's why you keep going with your education so you can find the job you like and that you are prepared for!"

One of the students I am still in touch with had a baby in the nursery. She was smart and had so much potential. She was doing really well at our school when she lost the place she was living in and had to move just across the boundary for our school district. It was going to be temporary as she was trying to get a place close-by again. I knew if she dropped out of school, she might never come back, so I did what I needed to do to keep her with us; I picked her and her baby up every morning for several months so she could stay in school. I never told anyone and I'm glad I did what I did. By the way, I used a proper baby seat in the car. Safety first!

On one of those drives, my student, Anna, was talking about the mistakes she had made and how her life was ruined because she didn't think she could ever go to college. I told her the greatest and most difficult job in the world was being a parent and doing it well. Anna graduated from high school and moved on with her life.

Years later, I delight in her life and what she has accomplished. She continues to be a great mom. During our current Covid-19 Pandemic, Anna has risen to the challenge of being teacher as well as mom. She helps her children do their lessons during this difficult time and she's good at it.

As teachers we have such a big responsibility to our students, not only in teaching them the curriculum, but in guiding them through the ups and downs life throws at them. Many days the job is difficult and comes with failure, but on those wonderful days when everything goes well, the reward is tremendous. It is especially rewarding to be in touch with former students and know they are doing well. And if they still need a little advice from me, I'm happy to be there for them.

Popcorn and Groups

A few years after I started teaching at the high school, the school psychologist and I decided we should start a group so the students could talk about issues that impacted them. The group would consist of any student who wanted to participate, the school psychologist and me. My two aides were also present. Our group would meet once a week.

I was fortunate to have a sink and countertop area in my room where a microwave I purchased, a small refrigerator and a coffee pot resided. Sometimes students had not eaten breakfast, so I kept fresh fruit in a basket and fresh coffee at the ready. For group time, I would occasionally microwave popcorn. This gave the room a good smell and a sense of comfort.

Group always started with these words. "Whatever is said here stays here. The exceptions are if you are being harmed or if anyone is threatening to harm you or someone else. At that time, an adult will get you help by reporting what was said to an outside authority."

This is similar to 12 step program sayings, but not exactly the same. The students knew and accepted the rule.

Surprisingly, whatever was said inside group never made the gossip rounds at school or outside of school, as far as I know. The students felt safe with us and would open up about situations at home or with questions about relationships. The wonderful thing that happened was other students shared similar situations and how they had handled it, which helped the student with the problem.

Sometimes there was laughter and sometimes tears, but always a sense of letting go and sharing with like-minded students and open-minded adults. It was also a bonding time for all of us.

Try to make your room warm and welcoming with any extras you can afford to provide. Students will want to come in and work and maybe even stay after school for tutoring and working on assignments, including my favorite, writing.

In today's climate of food allergies, check to see if your district prohibits the serving of food in the classroom.

Providing students with a safe environment where they can open up and share what is going on with them is important for the ability to learn. We ourselves know when things are bothering us as adults, it's sometimes hard to concentrate. It's the same with students, so make your room the place your students feel safe. Then they are the most receptive to learning.

Chocolate Chip Cookie Day

There were days where nothing seemed to work. The lesson had been planned, materials gathered, teacher and aides prepped and ready to teach. The students had shown up physically, but mentally weren't available.

Some days if I pushed too hard, the students became anxious or downright hostile. My aides and I became frustrated. On those days, students were told to work on independent assignments. The lesson planned for that day was held for another one when the students were receptive.

Since my aides and I had little control of our young scholars, we did what we could by cleaning our room. We would start organizing our desks and then the book shelves or some other area of the room. Looking around we'd see what the other one was doing and laugh at our like-mindedness.

Those were also the days that one of my aides would declare a *Chocolate Chip Cookie Day* for each of us during nutrition or break time. Not so nutritious, but quite warm and comforting. We had a great cafeteria cookie maker at our school and we took advantage of her on days like that.

Those were also the days that had us conferencing after school trying to dissect the problems keeping students from engaging with the lesson. Some days we figured it out and many days we didn't have a clue. We hoped things would be better the next day, but in the meantime, our room was spotless.

Don't hesitate to take a step back and reassess the lesson; talk to the students and find out what the problem was that day so changes can be made for the future.

If need be, make it a *Chocolate Chip Cookie Day* for the purpose of comfort and sanity.

Music Hath Charms...

The quote often attributed to William Shakespeare, but actually written by William Congreve, *Music hath charms to soothe a savage beast*, held great meaning in my classes.

Music was used when I taught elementary school to calm the students returning from recess and lunch. It was equally effective with secondary students during those times, and also used in lessons to illustrate a time period, as it did when teaching lessons provided by PBS and TNT. Writing as well as music was an integral part of these units or lessons.

Besides my regular assignment as an RSP teacher, I was given the honor of directing a choir. I had benefited from choirs and music most of my life, so through the years–seven of them–the sometimes large, sometimes small choirs, performed at senior centers and hospitals for the holidays and at other times.

One year, when the choir was larger, we performed a musical written for schools called *The Elephant's Child*, by Rudyard Kipling. We visited several elementary schools with this one, and our next production, which was an adaptation of the musical, *Grease*, by Jim Jacobs and Warren Casey.

I learned to have understudies for the major parts since there was a tendency for student absences on performance days. The musical *Grease,* was a major undertaking, but the rehearsals went well and we were ready.

On the day of the performance, my main female lead was absent, but her understudy, Liz, was present, so I wasn't too concerned. In addition, two boys from the chorus never made it. But the show must go on, and it did.

The next day when the two missing boys came to school, this was what they said,

"We got arrested and had to spend the night in jail. The officers didn't believe us when we told them we were in a musical and they needed to let us go. They just laughed."

These boys were sorry and made it for the next two performances. Music and responsibility became important to those *savage beasts*.

Again, as teachers, we learn to use everything in our arsenals to reach and hold on to our students. Never forget the impact music can have on your students.

Belonging to something and being responsible for the success of an enterprise you've invested in are powerful tools. In many cases my students had never been trusted with being part of a program that required practicing for many weeks and then participating in a performance. The fact that those boys made it to all the other performances demonstrates the importance of trusting their commitment. See if doing something like I did helps your students mature into the commitments they made.

Dark Humor and More

There were many times in my career I used humor to lighten the mood and get through the day. I'll share two of them with you.

The first one has to do with classroom behavior–not mine–the students' behavior. This was at the high school level. They loved to gossip! They loved drama! The more salacious, the better. So, when they were working on assignments and allowed to chat among themselves, the drama and gossip was sometimes at a very high level.

To backtrack a bit, I was once visiting a friend from my high school days when I noticed a can of room deodorizing spray on top of her refrigerator. It had an interesting title and laughingly I said, "I could use that spray in my classroom when things get out of hand!" She gave it to me.

Back to the drama and gossip–the can of spray was now in my desk, lower drawer on the right, when I heard the conversation get totally out of hand regarding unverified gossip. I opened the drawer, took out the spray and proceeded to spray around the table of the talkers. It actually smelled pretty good, something like cinnamon. I didn't say anything, but let the students see the label on the can. It said, "B*** S*** Spray!" I got the reaction I wanted–they laughed and got back to work.

From then on, when the drama accelerated, all I had to do was open the drawer, pull out the spray and threaten to use it. They always laughed and moved on!

And, another one. At the winter holiday season, our partner in education enabled my choir to go to various Sr. Citizen homes and hospitals to sing and hopefully bring some joy to the residents. During one of those visits to a retirement home, we pulled up in our bus and were getting ready to disembark when some of the students noticed a coroner's van parked at the curb and then two individuals wheeling a loaded gurney toward the van.

Some of the girls started screaming. I said over and over, "Look at me, just look at me! Everything is going to be okay!"

They calmed down, we did our performance, which was pretty good considering the circumstances, and we made it back to school.

Later, when I was sitting exhausted in the teacher's room trying to unwind, the principal came in and asked how the performance went.

I replied, "Just fine, they were dying to see us!"

Some other things that come to mind in those 30 years of teaching are the times I tried to encourage students and support them. I once took a student to an Al-Anon meeting so she could see and feel the kind of help she needed to deal with a tough situation at home. She continued to attend and she told me the meetings were helping her understand her family dynamics.

I also visited one of my students in a mental hospital after she had had a breakdown. It surprised her that I came, but ultimately helped our teacher/student relationship when she got out and came back to school.

A student in junior high school moved away the last year of school but we kept in touch by letter. One of the letters I received from him was from prison. He was much older now, had gotten in trouble and was paying for it. I kept writing until there were no more letters from him.

Even now, many years later, I still wonder what happened and why he stopped writing. I hope he's okay and got his act together so he could live a good life.

As teachers, we do what we have to do to keep our sanity and the sanity of our students. Humor, sometimes dark humor, helps the situation, helps the students and helps us, their teachers to be able to keep going.

We don't know what circumstances and situations will present themselves to us as we begin our teaching careers. Look at what teachers have had to do during our Covid-19 Pandemic. No one saw that coming, but my goodness, the creativity of teachers is astounding! Teachers rose to the situation and created unbelievable lessons to help students learn from home. Hats off to all of you! I am so impressed with your dedication in trying to reach your students.

Overcoming Nerves

My official title was Resource Specialist and as I've said before, my program was called Resource Specialist Program–RSP for short. That meant I was to work with students who had learning disabilities. They could have reading difficulties like dyslexia or problems with processing information, as in mathematics. Students could be dysgraphic, meaning having difficulty with writing. And, there were other disabilities under the RSP umbrella, mainly dealing with processing problems.

But in reality, at my school, it meant I could have students with many other problems, from being physically handicapped, visually and or hearing impaired to emotional disorders. It's probably quite the same way for some of you at your school or with your own child.

It was okay; I never wanted to turn anyone away.

Rachael was coming to the school in two weeks. My aides and I were nervous when told about her. She was confined to a wheelchair and could not go to the bathroom on her own as her weakness prevented her from doing so; which meant we had to learn how to help her use the toilet. This accounted for the nervousness we had. We didn't want to make any mistakes or make her feel uncomfortable.

A district nurse came to school with equipment and demonstrated how to help Rachael. A platform with an arm was set up in the nurse's office. It worked by being moved over the wheelchair. Strong clips attached to a sling under Rachael were clipped to the arm and a crank was turned so the arm could lift her up and move her over the toilet.

Our uneasiness was put to rest the day Rachael arrived. She was a sweet, gentle girl and instantly accepting of us. She had been doing the toilet thing much longer than we had and helped us through the process until it became second nature for us too.

Rachael was a brilliant girl. She ended up tutoring many of the students in our class in all subjects including writing, as well as completing her own studies.

Rachael was an asset to the program and taught me to remain open to the differences even I wasn't familiar with. It was a good learning lesson I tried to remember for the rest of my career as I worked with exceptional students. We, as human beings and teachers, want to improve our students lives and hopefully, we do. What I learned during my years of teaching is that our students enrich our lives too, and as I look back on my career, I realize how much my life was enhanced by the students I was honored to teach.

One Word Can Change Everything

Sometimes the simplest word will open doors with students. Read on to see how it worked for me one time.

A prospective student was facing assessment to see if he could benefit from being in my Resource Specialist Program.

Because I had read his cumulative record, the only thing I knew about him was that he was from a European country and had been in an orphanage. Having been adopted by an American couple when in the primary grades, he was now at our school because of little progress at the regular high school.

Pulling Kevin out of art class so I could assess him for the program, I felt his anger immediately. I could almost see the chip on his shoulder.

Thanking him for coming with me, I then said in the language of the country he was from, "Thank You."

He stopped walking and looked at me quizzically.

"How do you know that word?" he asked.

I told him I had learned it when hosting students from a student exchange program.

His mood lightened as he asked me to tell him about the experience of hosting students.

When I finished, he told me a little about his life in his birth country.

We made it through the assessment and he did qualify for the program. He was an active participant in all his classes and eventually graduated.

It's amazing how one word, or two, from a teacher, can change a student's attitude and the direction of their educational journey.

Do your research on your students. If you are one of those teachers who reads their Cumulative Records–Cums–before the school year starts, or waits a few weeks until they have been in your class a while, read the Cums. You find out so much from what other teachers have said about them and it can help you help them. It might even give you a hint as to the one or two words that can change your students path in school like it did with me and my student.

Lifelong Connections

She was a hot mess. Coming from a different district to live with her mom and stepdad, Tammy clearly didn't want to be at my school, yet here she was. At the time, I didn't know what the family circumstances were that led to her being here.

I found out she had had a serious injury when quite young and that injury kept her from retaining information, therefore the reason for being in my class. She was not quite 16 years old.

How was I going to help this beautiful young woman? She settled in fairly well at first but problems at home continued to get in the way.

Consistency when working with students is important. Also helping them to understand that you are there for them no matter what is of utmost importance. That is what I did for Tammy during the time she was at the school.

Because of memory issues, I gave her a notebook where she could write down anything she felt was important, from dates of meetings to homework assignments. She carried that notebook everywhere. In fact, she still uses that technique today more than twenty years later–but I'm getting ahead of the story of Tammy.

Tammy completed almost two years of school with me, but dropped out and returned to her original district. The problems with her family kept her from graduating.

There was something so special about her and I wanted to help in any way I could, so we kept in touch. Remember what I said about being there for your students no matter what? Remember consistency?

It worked out that Tammy came back. She couldn't attend our school, but she could attend the local adult school and she worked hard to complete her education. She graduated with her high school diploma and I was there to see her do that.

We have continued to talk through the years and text more often. I treasure that contact. I will always be there for her if she needs me. Consistency, no matter what! And, guess what, she is there for me too. We talk politics and commiserate about life. I enjoy our conversations but I still have her call me Forletta, which is what she called me when in my program. It feels right.

You will, as teachers, build connections with your students–some more than others. In many cases, you will be the glue that holds a student together and moves them in the right direction so they can live their best life.

When I shared what I had written about her, she told me a story.

She said, "I thought you were cool as a teacher. One day I tried to hide how sad I was but you noticed and took me out in the hall where I started to cry. A friend of mine had died and I was devastated. You sat down on the floor in the hallway next to me and held me.

Thank you for doing that."

It's important to be there for your students when they are sad and when they celebrate important milestones. They won't forget and neither will you.

Keeping Students Safe

As teachers we know things pile up. There are papers to correct and grade, reports to write and meetings to schedule; lessons to plan and those bulletin boards that take extra time are always on your mind. That's why I would come to school early.

Inevitably, those were also the days something else would pop up to make well-laid plans disappear. One day I arrived early to finish scoring an assessment and write the report for the meeting scheduled for later that day. Well into the process at my desk, the door opened and in came one of my students who was behind in his work.

I said, "Hi Greg. You're here early. What's up?"

He replied, "I thought I'd catch up on my assignments."

He got his textbook and paper and sat down.

I continued with my report, but noticed he wasn't doing anything and kept wiping at his face. His head was down, but now I noticed a bruise on the side of his face, so I went to sit next to him.

I said, "Look at me."

When he did, I could see he had a black eye developing and another bruise on his forehead besides the one on the side of his face. Tears were running down his cheeks. At first, he wouldn't tell me what had happened. After some back and forth he finally said he and his dad had been in an argument and his face was the end result.

As teachers we are the protectors of our students and by law, we have to report injury and abuse. I convinced Greg to walk to the office with me where we talked to the principal. She let me know she would take care of it and invited the student to stay with her.

These things happen–even on the days we are overwhelmed with reports that need to be written. The principal and I made sure he was going to be safe and the correct legal avenues pursued. Counseling from our school psychologist was also initiated.

By a miracle, I was able to finish the report and make it to the meeting later in the day. This is the life of a teacher. There are some who say, "Those who can, do. Those who can't, teach." On the other hand, I say, "Spend a day, or if you are really brave, spend a week in the classroom of a teacher and then perhaps revise that comment!"

If You See Something, Say Something

The lessons for the study of the Holocaust lasted many weeks. It was a schoolwide event specifically for students in Social Studies classes, but open to others who were interested in elective credits. Another teacher and I were in charge of this very sensitive subject.

The preparations included a brief study of the circumstances leading up to World War II. We also had a selection of books relating to the war that were available for students to read and finish with a book report before our joint studies began.

We received parental permission for students to watch *Schlinder's List*, 1993, directed and produced by Steven Spielberg and written by Steven Zaillian, as well as inviting survivors and liberators to share their experiences with the students during an assembly. This was difficult and often the first time these senior citizens had shared their stories. Many students were in tears.

A field trip to the *Museum of Tolerance*, in Los Angeles, California, was another activity and an eye opener for many, even the ones who were of the belief the Holocaust was a myth. Discussions and writing assignments rounded out the study.

During one of the smaller group discussions held in my room, two of my students were very open about how the study had affected them because they felt *different*.

One female student named Alicia said, "You don't know what it's like to be Hispanic in this community we live in. I'm harassed constantly."

Another boy responded with, "I have three things against me; I'm black, I'm fat, and I'm gay. Can you imagine the prejudice I feel every day?"

In my class, students were accepted for who they were, but out on the street, out in the world, these young people had a difficult time. I could only encourage them and all the students to understand the saying, "If you see something, say something. We can't let what happened in the Holocaust happen here."

It was a lesson reinforced by our tour guide at the *Museum of Tolerance* when he said the same thing to all of us, "If you see something, say something!"

I hoped the lessons about the Holocaust changed students in ways that made them more tolerant of each other and their differences. Things, in my opinion, aren't much better since that time in my class and lessons on tolerance and acceptance continue to be important. As teachers in the classroom, it is important for you to find ways to open your students' hearts and minds.

Teachers today are faced with challenges of every kind. Racism, global warming, political discord, homelessness, a Covid-19 Pandemic, to name just a few. The responsibility placed on you as educators is immense. But the opportunity you have to shape the future of your students is yours to discover. I believe you all have the ability, creativity and sensitivity to help your students understand themselves and our world and try to make it a better, safer place.

Never Give Up

Two of my students had great difficulty with writing when they first came to my class. Harry was extremely dyslexic–difficulty with reading, and dysgraphia–problems with writing. When doing standardized testing, his Individualized Educational Plan, IEP, allowed the test to be read to him. His auditory and verbal comprehension was good, but he had little desire to write because of his disabilities. He was however, brilliant when it came to mathematical equations.

Then, there was Tommy, who came to my room from the local high school, sat himself in a corner and kept his head lowered to his chest. When given assignments, he would sit and attempt to complete the assignments but never ask for help. I would go to him, sit and ask, "Need help?"

He usually said, "No."

Rather than walking away one day, I stayed and talked. I told him about myself and the different schools where I had been employed prior to coming to the high school. I also talked about all the different grades I had taught. Other soliloquies on my part dealt with my children, my dogs and anything else I could think to mention.

Occasionally I would ask for a response and if I got one, it was usually one or two words, but increased to more as time went on. Tommy had some emotional issues, but mainly had just been ignored most of his school career.

The reason I bring up these two young men is to encourage you to see beyond the problems of students who others think might not make it. Both of these students wanted an education and a chance to succeed in life.

My basic goal for Harry in writing was that he could pick out a greeting card, write a short message inside and give it to a loved one because he had asked for help with that task.

My basic goal for Tommy was for him to verbally communicate with classmates, teachers and family members.

Both basic goals, as well as all the others needed for graduation, were met thanks to the law allowing students with disabilities to remain in high school beyond the age of 18. They both graduated from our high school.

I knew both young men were employable if given the chance and it has been 20 plus years later as I write this and both men are still employed and the main wage earners for their families.

When graduation arrived at our school, students could volunteer to give a speech. Tommy asked if he could give one.

Here it is in its entirety: "Thank you Mrs. Forletta."

It was the best speech I ever heard!

Hold Them Near

Jimmy was a student of mine. He was one of those special kids that grabbed my heart right from the start. He had a quiet, gentle strength and bright, insightful, blue eyes. At eighteen, he was not yet as mature as he would be someday. And another thing, he was stubborn.

Jimmy would sit alone in the back of the room. But as time went by, he moved closer until he finally claimed the desk right beside mine. He was now close enough for me to quietly talk to him when he was hurting and needed a comforting word. Right in front of him was his very own special place to put his books and papers. It was a plastic bin and he would place his file folder in it when done working for the day. He didn't want to put his things in our regular file cabinet.

After a few weeks had gone by without Jimmy attending, I was worried he had dropped out in spite of phone calls home by me and the school office. It was midway through first period when I heard the sound of his car engine, and I knew he was back.

Jimmy walked in the door with his apologetic, gentle smile and said, "I'm sorry I haven't been here. I'm going to be more regular from now on. I want to graduate and I'm going into the military when I finish."

I answered with, "Welcome back Jimmy. I'm so glad to see you. I never gave up on you and I'm glad you're going to come every day so you can finish, graduate and go into the service."

Jimmy sat down and worked hard the whole day on World History and Economics. He went to Art for a period but came back to do English; his most difficult subject. When he started English with me, his writing was difficult to read and didn't always make sense. He took home a typed book report to show his parents. It was good and made sense–his best work so far. He was proud of that report and so was I! He was making progress.

When school was over, Jimmy assured me he would be back the next day. I sighed inside and prayed he would be. I then made the decision to pick Jimmy to take to the Dodger game that year. Each year at our school, all members of the staff would pick a student they felt had made progress and reward them with seeing a Dodger game. Jimmy loved baseball. The year before I took someone else and Jimmy was curious about the activity and wanted to try for the honored spot.

At graduation, forty students participated. If Jimmy had been on target with his classes and credits, he would have graduated too. Instead, last week I participated in another kind of traditional ceremony for Jimmy—his funeral. In the newspaper article that talked about the car crash on the rainy day he died, they called him a man because he was eighteen. He was really just a sweet kid.

I miss Jimmy with his gentle soul and quiet, shy smile. I never got to tell him about the baseball game.

Sometimes life intervenes and reminds us as teachers to hold on to our students as best we can and help them while we have the chance.

In Conclusion

Positive and negative influences in our lives help to make us who we are. As humans we experience both. How we choose to use those experiences is what guides us in our lives.

Some of the negative influences ultimately helped me be a better, more understanding teacher. For example, the kindergarten teacher who walked around the room with a yardstick in her hand. When we were sitting at our desks working on an assignment, we were not allowed to talk. One day the boy behind me whispered something to his neighbor. The teacher smashed his hand with the yardstick. To this day, I remember his scream. I learned not to talk.

When I was in the 3rd grade, I contracted Rheumatic Fever and was home for six months. I eventually had a teacher, toward the end of that time, come to my house with a few lessons but I missed quite a lot in that six months. So, when I returned to school something happened that was very impacting on me as a student and ultimately as a teacher.

It was math time and the teacher had put some problems on the board. He called a few students at a time up to the board to solve them. When it was my turn, I tried to solve what I thought was a subtraction problem. When I couldn't figure it out, I whispered to the teacher that I needed help with my problem.

He stopped the whole class and said, "Class, class, can I have your attention? Barbara can't figure out how to solve her *subtraction* problem!"

The class erupted into laughter as they studied the board. It turned out what I was trying to solve was not subtraction, but an addition problem with three rows of numbers; one on top of the other. To this day, I remember the humiliation. I learned not to volunteer in class.

Those negative incidents stayed with me and I hope I never inflicted something like what I had experienced upon my students. It shuts down the student and the learning.

In contrast, Mr. Hillman was encouraging and helpful to all students in junior high algebra class, including me, as I constantly struggled with math. His influence taught me to be the same to my students when they were struggling.

And then finally, while waiting to board a flight at Los Angles International Airport, I saw a yogurt cart and decided to buy one as I waited for my flight. I ordered a vanilla, but the young lady just looked at me.

She asked, "Are you a teacher?"

"Yes," I replied.

"Are you Mrs. Forletta?" she asked.

It turned out Elizabeth had been in my 5th grade class in inner city, Los Angeles. Do you remember earlier in the book how I talked about how difficult that year of teaching had been for me and realizing that in order to stay in teaching I would have to find another position? What a wonderful coincidence to run into her and talk about that year.

When Elizabeth's shift was over, she joined me at the table where I sat. She shared that she was working on her teaching credential. She said she was going into teaching because of me.

"I wanted to make a difference in a child's life like you made a difference in mine," she said.

Even though I thought I hadn't done a very good job teaching those students in inner city, I guess somehow, my efforts had made an impact.

You see how as teachers we shape student's lives? Some incidents are negative and some positive. I remembered the negative episodes and hopefully made sure I didn't inflict anything like those on my students. I remembered the positive ones and used those to uplift my students. You have a variety of experiences in your own lives, so use them to be better teachers.

I hope this book will give your students more of the positive events to embrace. Perhaps then, they too can go out into the world to shape those they come in contact with in a positive manner.

Good luck and have fun!

Appendix

Parts of an Essay
Student worksheet

Introduction

Explain to the reader what you're going to tell them in an opening paragraph.

At the end of your introduction/opening paragraph, introduce your *Thesis*.

The *Thesis* is the main focus of the essay and is an idea or feeling about the topic/subject.

Body

Tell the reader. Give detailed information.

Have at least three or more paragraphs–more is better.

This is the extension and focus of the *Thesis*.

Conclusion

Tell the reader what you told them in this final paragraph.

You are restating or summarizing.

This final paragraph is a good place for personal observation or reflection about the topic/subject.

Book Report Form

The following information will guide you in creating your book report.

Title

Author

Main Characters

Minor Characters

Illustrator

Publisher

Setting–Where and when did it take place?

Plot–What happens and in what order?

Conflict–What are the problems within the story and with the characters? How are the problems solved?

Theme–Does the author express his/her point of view or reason for writing the story so that you understood it? What was the author's point-of-view?

Reaction–How did the story affect you?

If you have an idea about a different way to do your book report, come and talk to me about it. Some other ideas are:

A letter from one character to another.
Writing a different ending to the story.
Designing a book cover for your book.

You can add to your book report and receive extra credit by doing more of the above suggested assignments.

Multi Media Permission Slip

Dear Parent/Guardian,

In our class this semester/quarter, we are viewing the media/online resources listed below:

_____

_____

_____

_____

_____

Our theme for the semester/quarter is _____ _____

We will be doing a variety of activities including journal writing, art projects, online research, reading and writing projects on the subject.

By signing below, you are giving your permission for your son or daughter to participate in the activities for this class.

If you have any questions, please feel free to call, text or email me at:

_____

Thank you,

_____

_____   _____

Parent Signature   Date

Project Resources

Student Handout

Internet
>Search Engines: Google, Yahoo, etc.
>www.historychannel.com
>www.discoverychannel.com
>Encyclopedia Britannica: www.search.eb.com
>Any other online source–appropriate and verifiable

Hardcopy Encyclopedia–current edition

Books on your subject

Library

Bookstores

Museums and Museum Bookstores

Movies/Online resources/Television specials/documentaries on your topic

Teachers, parents, other authorities on your topic

Student Essay

Although I did not include a lesson on PBS's *Colonial House* in the lessons in this book, I wanted to demonstrate how the writing of many drafts improve students' work. This writing is from that lesson and although the final draft is not perfect, you can see the improvement.

First is the original draft from the PBS television presentation. Both versions are as written by the student with all mistakes left in place. The final version was after two more revisions. Remember, the goal is to take students as they are and help them improve their skills. I used italics to emphasize the writing. The student used regular type.

First Draft

As a class we watch the movie the "Colonial House." It was about how people lived in the 1600's. they lived very different from the way people live today. Things have changed in so many ways.

In people lives today they have so much. They don't have to heat water to take a bath. All they have to do is turn the nozzle one way and you get hot/warm water for their bath! We start fires in the fire place cause they look pretty to watch. Cooking for us is much easier. We can eat food that does not even need to be cooked. They did also, but they would have to pick it. We can buy ours. We have so many thing they did not have we have make-up they don't. We buy are milk they don't they milk the cow

There are many more things that have changed.

I am sure in another 200 years things will be different. It is crazy how things change over the years.

Final Draft

The 17th Century vs. Now

As a class, we watched the PBS Video, <u>The Colonial House.</u> It was about how people lived in 1628. They lived very differently from the way people live today. Things have changed in so many different ways. I showed this change by making a collage to symbolize those different ways.

People today have too much. They don't have to heat water to take a bath. All they have to do is turn the nozzle one-way and you get hot/warm water. The colonists had to go chop down wood so they could cook, make the hot/warm water for their bath. We start fires in the fireplace because they look pretty to watch and not so much for heat.

Cooking is much easier for us too. We can eat food that does not even need to be cooked. It's pre-cooked. In a way they did too, but they would have to grow it and harvest it, like the corn they grew. We just go to the store and buy it.

We have so many things they did not have. We have make-up. They didn't. They had animals that give milk. We just go to the store and buy it. There are so many more things. Just look at my college.

I am sure in another 200 years, things will be different and students then will be comparing their lives to mine. It is crazy how things change over years.

About the Author

Barbara Bush Forletta inherited the joy of reading and writing from her mom June. In the 1970s, Barbara began writing an annual Christmas letter and those letters have become a historical record of her family. Chronicling her family's personal history, Barbara wrote *Lifetimes* in 2015. She also wrote an article detailing life as a host family for American Field Service, an exchange student program, which was published in 2000 in the AFS International Newsletter. Her exchange students came from Finland, Germany and Spain and lived with the family for a year each.

In 1995, The Library of Congress National Library of Poetry included one of Barbara's poems in an anthology. She is also published in two anthologies from the Golden Pen Writers Guild, *Writing Out Loud* and *This and That*.

Barbara began her 30-year teaching career as an elementary teacher. While teaching, she went back to CSU, Northridge, California to earn her Special Education Credential and taught students with a variety of challenges at the middle and high school levels.

Barbara's credentials, certificates and experience include:

     Clear Multiple Subject/Ryan-Life

     Learning Handicapped Specialist/Clear

     Resource Specialist Certificate of Competence/Clear

     Specifically Designed Academic Instruction in English Certificate of Completion

     Consulting Teacher; PAR/BUSD

     Support Provider BTSA/Induction Program/Burbank Unified School District

     No Child Left Behind Certificate of Compliance

     State of Nevada License for Educational Personnel

     Supervising Mentor Teacher, Elementary School, State of Nevada

     Teacher of the Year, Monterey High School, BUSD 2003-2004

Barbara's current writing focus is the documenting of life during the Covid 19 Pandemic and the current nature of democracy in the United States.

In her free time, Barbara enjoys Mah-jongg, reading, gardening and playing handbells in her church choir. She has two children and many grandchildren. She loves and adores them all!

Barbara can be reached through email at barbaraforletta@gmail.com

Teacher Notes

Teacher Notes

Teacher Notes

Teacher Notes

Made in the USA
Las Vegas, NV
19 June 2022

50431128R00077